To Lynn—

outside
looking
in

You are never on
your own'.
keep in touch.

Ant.

To Lynne,

You are never on your own.
Love you loads.

Ana.

outside looking in

Audrey Clark

Matador
9 Priory Business Park,
Wistow Road, Kibworth Beauchamp,
Leicestershire. LE8 0RX
Tel: (+44) 116 279 2299
Fax: (+44) 116 279 2277
Email: books@troubador.co.uk
Web: www.troubador.co.uk/matador

ISBN 978 178306 110 5

British Library Cataloguing in Publication Data.
A catalogue record for this book is available from the British Library.

Typeset by Troubador Publishing Ltd, Leicester, UK

Matador is an imprint of Troubador Publishing Ltd

Printed and bound in the UK by TJ International, Padstow, Cornwall

MIX
Paper from
responsible sources
FSC
www.fsc.org
FSC® C013056

*For the silent survivors. There are too many of us,
and it's time we spoke out.*

CONTENTS

FOREWORD

When I read personal accounts of harrowing events it seems that the individuals concerned always come through the other end or their account becomes a rag-to-riches story. Mine doesn't. It's an on-going process with good days and bad days. I have tried to be honest. I am conscious that my thought processes suggest confusion or lack of clarity but trust me when I say they were very clear to me, each and every one of them when they occurred. I only skim the surface. I know that.

That's due to fear. I hold back because at times events however scantily portrayed are harrowing for me and I deal with that by skimming the surface.

As for being rich, well, I do think being 'rich' can be defined in a number of ways. Having good health makes me feel rich. The love of those closest makes me feel particularly rich. If you are thinking this book will chart harrowing events followed by a happy ending then you may be disappointed. I have written this book to inform you, the reader, in the hope it may resonate with some.

Whilst you may not have had my experiences you may know people who have. Reading this may frustrate you. It may sadden you or at times it may make you smile. It has been a cathartic process for me. If you are a survivor then I applaud you. There are many of us whose actions are misunderstood. If you are reading this and have been a victim and continue to keep it a secret then that's your choice but to me it's a disease and my antibiotic is gleaned by writing my account. Please don't suffer in silence. Just tell one other person and you lighten the load. Trust me.

Obstacles ARE the building blocks to success.

Aud Clark
March 2013

CHAPTER ONE

THE MONSTER WITHIN

Salford in the North West of England is famous for being the birth place of the iconic artist L.S Lowry, renowned for his match stick figures. It is also the town where I was born and spent the first ten years of my life. Ironically, after moving back to the town in 1996 I now live minutes away from Lowry's former home on Station Road in Swinton.

I was born on 20 June 1963 to a German mother, Christa Anneliese Ehliger, and a British father, Harold Yates, at Hope Hospital in Salford. Whilst I don't remember that day I do recall my mum recounting a story that whilst in hospital the nurse said: "If you carry on feeding her like that she'll be carrying you out and not the other way around!"

A somewhat chubby baby with a hearty appetite I had one half-brother, John. He was nine years older than me and was born in Toronto, Canada. My mum's first born following a tempestuous affair with Mike, a Polish businessman who dumped her on finding out she was expecting. It was 1954. Illegitimate births were frowned upon, as was alcoholism. As a boy on public transport John piped up: "My mom drinks beer you know!" The odd beer, I hasten to add, and not frequently. Some shook their heads in dismay at the revelation. My mum hastily grabbed his arm, pulling him towards the exit as fellow passengers frowned.

Mum and dad were pen-pals in the real sense of the word. It was too early for emails or smart phones then. Following a paper courtship mum moved to Salford from Germany and became Christa Yates. This was a second marriage for my father, who was sixteen years her senior at the age of fifty-one. His first marriage dissolved on the grounds of extreme cruelty. Obviously, my mother didn't know that when she agreed to marry him.

My earliest Salford memories were in the local sweet shop sat on a long, dark, wooden counter. The shopkeeper looked like Arkwright from *Open All Hours*. He was a man in his late 50s wearing a white coat. He was bespectacled with a receding hair line and a warm smile inviting me to reach in and sample the contents.

Happy, happy days…

Happy memories were not the norm, sadly. What unfolded was a childhood spent treading on egg-shells trying not to upset 'him' – my father. I call him that because there was no love there, nothing in fact except emptiness.

He neither earned my love nor deserved it. When he died in

1984 I shed not one tear. Nor did I attend his funeral. I was void of all feeling.

In fact the last time I saw him was following a very final goodbye as a feisty fourteen year old, but more of that later. My emotions had become so distorted I felt like I was looking at myself in the hall of mirrors. I saw nothing of my beauty, instead I saw a distorted image that bore no reflection to the real me, the inner me.

My mum, bless her, now she was a serious woman. Tall, slender and intelligent, she possessed a dry wit. A typical Capricorn goat climbing the mountain slowly and steadily, battling all the elements thrown at her with fortitude and tenacity. She suffered for most of that time at the hands of my father but when she shone she could rival the brightest star on any Christmas tree. Her witty repartee and smile were her most endearing qualities. She was enviously slim.

My father? Well, he was a nasty, vile man. He was of slight build. Five feet eight inches tall. A truly controlling monster, but to the outside world he upheld the persona of an amiable, helpful and generous man. To mum, John and I he was angry, violent, cruel and cantankerous ninety-nine per cent of the time. He was an abusive man. I feel nothing when I think of him. I believed the years would mellow me but his vile, physical and systematic abuse of me from the tender age of seven made my ability to feel impossible.

Mum worked as a typist and translator at John Myers Catalogue Company in Eccles, Manchester. The company folded in the mid-1980s. Mum would walk in all weathers for an hour every morning to get to work, having only enough bus fare for the journey one way. Oh, not because she didn't earn enough. She did. But because he took the majority of her earnings almost as soon as her weekly pay packet was opened for inspection whilst his wage as a school caretaker at St Saviours Primary School, in Kearsley sat gaining interest in his bank account. The house was usually cold unless he was there. He would sit warming his hands at the three-bar electric fire. My mum sat in the corner wearing a thick cardigan.

We had a pet mongrel called Blackie. A lively, intelligent dog. He quickly picked up on impending violence, edging his way closer to her side. If she went upstairs he did too. If she sat weeping he was there sat with her. He tried in his own way to comfort her. He was her protector, her support.

We lived in a three-bedroom, mid-terraced council property on Carrfield Grove, Little Hulton, Worsley. A kind, elderly couple called Mr and Mrs Cole lived next door. They were a lovely couple who always had time for me. Across from us in the retirement bungalows lived a spritely, cheery, old woman in her late eighties known as Mrs Gardener. I always found her name funny as a kid because she really loved her garden and she was always pruning her pink-and-red roses to perfection with her trusty secateurs. She appeared to be out there in all weathers.

Back at home there was never enough to eat. As children we were always hungry. When I say we I mean Mum, John and I. He, however, ate like a king. Succulent roasts, mouth-watering chops, vegetables and puddings with a soup starter whilst we never had more than meagre rations. Toast seemed to be a staple part of my diet, along with baked beans or tinned 'something' in woefully inadequate amounts. My overriding memory of meal times is not the sense of hunger and a constant rumbling stomach. No, it was chomping. Not only did we not eat adequately but also had to endure the revolting sounds of his chomping of every mouthful of food. To this day I cannot sit next to anyone who chomps food.

I remember fainting one morning before school. I must have been out cold for no more than a couple of minutes. As I slowly came around I could see my mum's concern and guilt as she gently tapped my face and called out my name in an attempt to fully rouse me. I'm guessing I went straight to school after that as taking time off was not an option. I do remember still feeling hungry and unsteady on my feet when I was in assembly that morning.

Clearly there had been no additional food for me before leaving for school. When I wasn't fainting through hunger I was screaming. The tears were streaming down my face as I struggled for breath. I was on the verge of hyper-ventilating as he punched my mum, who was trying to protect her face with her hands while my brother tried in vain to pull him off, pleading with him to stop and getting hit himself in the process.

Blackie barked incessantly until he did. He never hit me. He shouted, yes, but never hit me. I was scared to death of him and I hated the pain he inflicted on those I loved. Many times I felt as though I was on the outside looking in, which was to become a pattern to be repeated many times throughout my life. I was just a child but I had a very different perception of family life and an innate awareness of impending violence and the stomach-churning feeling that it brought.

They say when you experience a traumatic experience your mind blocks it out for your protection and to a degree that's true, but it didn't quite block it out enough for me when one afternoon when I was aged just seven that protection theory was put to the test. It was mid-afternoon. I think it was the school holidays. I sat on the settee drawing. I was alone in the house with him. Mum was still at work. The atmosphere was calm. Almost too chilled, which may sound strange considering the atmosphere in the house most of the time. He came in from the kitchen which adjoined the living room carrying a mug of tea puffing on a Woodbine. He sat very close to me.

He was kind and nice. This was out of character for him. With foresight I should have guessed he had ulterior motives. Smiling and stroking my hair he told me how lovely I was. How pretty I was. One hand played with my shoulder length brown hair. I noticed his breathing was changing. He was excited. His other hand was just touching me above my knee. I was wearing a dress at the time. Next thing I knew he was kissing me on the neck under my ear. I wanted to scream. In my head I was screaming STOP! But my body was rigid with fear. What I remember next was being told how special I was and that this was our secret. His flies were undone and his erect, wet penis shook me to the core. What the hell was happening? Next thing I knew he was pushing me down onto the settee. "This is OUR SECRET. You mustn't tell anyone." Followed by the pain, agony and fear of being penetrated.

The tears began to flow and continue to flow to this day. As he approached orgasm he became kinder with his words, which made it a whole lot worse. He grunted and groaned until finally, mercifully, he had finished. He stood up, zipped his trousers and went into the kitchen to refresh his cup of tea whilst I lay there semi-naked with semen dripping out of me. On that day whether I liked it or not I became an adult and a victim. The hate I realised I had that day never left me. It intermittently erupts in varying ways right up to the current day. My actions make me ashamed sometimes but at least I know where they stem from and I know how to say sorry when I need to and trust me I say it a lot – but often too late to repair the damaged caused to the other person.

From that day on whenever he was in the mood he would refer to his 'doggie'. When he said that I knew sex with him was imminent.

As a child school was not just compulsory it became my saviour and protector. Peel Hall Junior School in Little

Hulton was a wonderful environment. The staff were so kind. They came to know me well, not least the caretaking staff who took me under their wing inviting me to the staff room nearly every morning for a cup of tea and a biscuit. You see I was dropped off an hour before school every morning so my mum could walk to work. I became the lone figure in the playground arriving even before Mr Seymour, the headmaster. He was a warm man. He was kind, strict and fair. He demonstrated the perfect combination of qualities for a teacher in charge. I came top of the class every Friday morning for the times table weekly test run by Mr Gregory, my form teacher, who helped me to discover the magic of Egypt, Tutankhamen and hieroglyphics. He was THE best teacher I have ever had. He encouraged and promoted my desire to learn.

After the trauma of child abuse, which was to be a burden of a secret, I then found myself in an ambulance at the age of eight, screaming, holding my right arm just above the elbow which was now gushing with blood. As I screamed out I remember being particularly upset that the new brown bubble coat I was wearing was well and truly ruined. Upsetting because it had been one of the few new items of clothing I had ever received. My clothes came from charity shops for most of my young life.

At the Bolton General Hospital I laid in casualty in intense pain. The doctor appeared in a long white coat which terrified me and began stitching my arm without much pain relief, as

I recall. I had also suffered concussion. The next four days spent in hospital were terribly traumatic for me. I cried inconsolably and incessantly. The nurses were so kind bringing chocolate, crayons and a book to take my mind off my hospital stay but nothing alleviated my upset apart from the visits from my mum.

I discovered from the driver of the Mini that hit me that I had crossed a main road to visit the sweet shop. I remember nothing of this. He was mortified. I enjoyed his box of Milk Tray though! Peering longingly through the mouth-watering assortment did take my mind off my confinement if only for a few minutes. I was also thrilled by a visit from the caretaker, who came on behalf of the school, clutching a mass of cards carrying one overriding message: 'You should have followed the Green Cross Code.'

Following my release – yes, it felt like prison with kindness – I recall being sat on the doorstep in the sunshine with my arm in a sling clutching my trophy stitches which were wrapped in cotton gauze. On return to school I sat eating lunch at the long wooden trestle table when Mr Seymour came over and gently nudged me to one side as he sat arms crossed, gently ticking me off for my lack of road safety awareness. Here was a male showing me genuine kindness and concern. Finding any male to look up to was rare for me and needless to say a moment I cherished. I just about recovered from that when I then found myself with our GP, Dr Solomon, sporting a nasty red scaly rash which almost appeared overnight. As I sat with my mum I vividly recall him telling my mum I had psoriasis. A rash with no known cure but one that needed continual cream and lotion application. So now as well as feeling different from my peers I would also look different. He surmised that the trauma of the car accident had brought on the condition. I wanted to scream out that the trauma wasn't the result of the accident but instead the result of the persistent abuse I endured.

Here was possibly the only chance I had to tell an adult. I was screaming inside 'Abuse! He abuses me', but the doctor could not hear my plea. I had lost my chance to have a responsible adult hear my plight and possibly save me from anything further happening in the future. Not long after my parents parted, albeit temporarily.

We moved to a furnished flat above a busy estate agent in Heaton Moor, Stockport. I can still picture the court official in a black gown crouching down to my level to ask 'Who do you want to live with, your mum or your dad?' Clutching my mum's hand ever so tightly the answer was an easy one. My mum! Here at last was respite for me from a harrowing, confusing and emotional time. The flat was cold. I didn't go to a new school and I remember eating cold beans from a can. I also remember the rare treat of bakery cakes. Sponge fingers filled with a sickly orange cream and being ill afterwards. I could relax for the first time in my young life. It was to be a temporary respite. Before very long he had charmed his way back in and we were in the same situation we had just left. I returned to my haven at Peel Hall, but that joy too was to be short lived as he informed us we were moving to Whitefield and another home on Selby Avenue.

So, here I was going to a new school in the very last year at my beloved junior school. I was without a doubt bereft. A part of me had indeed just died. My new school was probably OK, though I wouldn't have known as I spent every lunch break crying so I can't remember. They were painful days with the eleven plus examination sandwiched in for good measure just adding to the pressure. I passed the test, joining Stand Grammar School for Girls in Whitefield the following September to the pride of my father, who for once willingly put his hand in his pocket for the costly uniform from Weston's, the grammar schoolwear supplier.

I looked like a posh St Trinian with my long grey gabardine coat, navy blue uniform, red and navy tie and a grey bowler-type hat complete with elastic made to be pinged by the older girls intent on fun at the expense of a new girl. I never lived up to my parents' expectations there, though I was made a Vice House Captain before once again being wrenched away from school on what was to become the 'Great Escape'.

Would I ever feel settled and be able to anchor my roots? Would this now be an end to the abuse I had continually endured and would I ever be able to forgive my abuser?

CHAPTER TWO

THE GREAT ESCAPE

Now twelve years old my existence thus far had been one upheaval after another. It felt like I was on a fast-moving train with hardly any stops and then only momentary ones. I felt vulnerable and fragile. I clung to the few static people and places in my life, but as soon as I started to relax and enjoy my life the rug was swiftly pulled from under me.

I was changing. My hormones were raging. Experience had taught me to suppress emotion no matter how strongly I felt. I was the one on the outside looking in. It was like watching a film only I was now centre stage, powerless to change the ever-unfolding events taking place.

One night after school Mum and John told me to pack some belongings as we were leaving. I was told to take just what I needed. Clearly they had been planning it for a while. My father was away that night. This was our chance to be relinquished from his clutches. I knew the time to ask a question was not now so I set about packing.

The Great Escape was an event I remember more after I

arrived at my destination. Our home was to be in a small town in Northern Germany – Braunschweig – in May 1976. It's a 13th century town littered with black-and-white buildings indicative of the period. It resembled Chester in North West England, complete with the now familiar Tschibo coffee shops and an array of mouth-watering cake shops.

I was a poor traveller, the one vomiting in a carrier bag on a hot, stuffy coach. I would inhale the hairspray, pungent fragrance and constant cigarette smoke. No wonder I felt sick.

Mum, John and I were to leave late at night and head for the ferry to Holland, followed by an arduous onward trip to Braunschweig. The journey in total was some twenty-seven hours. I remember that. I was quite ill and somewhat dehydrated when we arrived. It was cold. I was tired. I was in a country where I could not speak the language. It was alien to me in every sense of the world. I was resentful. Once again the rug had been well and truly pulled from under me, adding to the mounting insecurity I felt. I suppose I should have been grateful. He couldn't get to us there. I was cold, tired, ill and in need of a bed.

My uncle Werner and aunt Eva had found us an apartment ten minutes from the town in a quiet, tree-lined complex known as Heinriche Heine Strasse. Sparsely furnished but clean and an acceptable base to begin our new life. The pressure was immediately on us to find work to sustain this new lifestyle. John was now twenty-one. He found temporary work quickly...in of all places an abattoir. We experienced the joy of eating warm, dead meat to complement our meagre rations.

Our weekly shopping list included:
    Land Brot – A dense, hard, dry, rye bread
    Citron tea – Granulated lemon tea
    Dry pasta
    And a bland, cheap margarine

It was truly awful. I discovered Lidl long before anyone else from the UK!

Mum found it difficult to find work. She had applied for jobs without success. A couple of polite refusals but no more than that usually. A glimmer of hope appeared with an interview a little distance from the apartment involving a thirty-minute walk. That was another theme. Walking. We walked everywhere as money was in short supply. John and I waited for her outside, kicking the gravel up in the hot summer sun. When Mum emerged it was pretty clear it hadn't gone too well. An occasional smoker, she reached for her matches and lit a cigarette. As she did, tucked neatly in the box folded in four, was a ten-mark note. Her interviewer had asked her for a light and slipped the note into the matchbox as thanks but no thanks. A kind gesture none the less.

My tennis pumps were ripped. Had it rained much it would have finally destroyed them. But, thankfully it was the hot summer of 1976, both in the UK and in Germany. I looked like a refugee. A down-and-out child. I was ashamed and embarrassed. I was very nearly a young woman. It was tough, very tough. I hated Germany but I understood the need to get as far away from him as possible.

My aunt and uncle were reasonably well off from what I could see. They had a third-floor apartment in a leafy nook with tall sash windows overlooking the park. The two cats would perch themselves on the window sill and bask in the sunshine as their giant black poodle Bingo would terrorise them relentlessly. He performed tricks like a sea lion at a show. I giggled at his antics playing dead dog. They also had a stunning summer house in the forest. This was my aunt's pride and joy surrounded by fruit bushes, humungous mushrooms and hiding places galore. My cousin, Thomas, was seventeen. He was cool and fun to be around as he tinkered with the rusty VW Beetle in preparation for passing an imminent driving test. He was the image of my aunt with the same red colouring and wry smile. My uncle on the other hand was plump and jovial but I later discovered his behaviour towards Eva had in the past mirrored that of my father towards my mother.

John introduced us to an old lady – Frau Boehme. She was a short, plump, courteous woman in her seventies. She was the grandmother of Manfred, a pen-pal John had formed a friendship with. She was very kind. She fed us handsomely on many occasions asking for nothing in return. Sometimes Mum would take cake on a visit. She appeared embarrassed to see her kindness being acknowledged. She was a lovely woman. She lived in a typical grandma-type apartment, china, lace and doilies everywhere. She was one in a million and so very hospitable. If she were alive today I would give her the biggest hug. She gave so much of herself to all of us, asking for nothing in return.

Summer came with a vengeance. It was SO hot that summer of 1976. Fashion there was dubious though. Everyone was wearing slip-on clogs. It was considered the item of footwear to be seen in. Personally I thought they were ugly and unbecoming. 'Mississippi' by the Pussycats rode the charts for weeks and weeks there.

It was also the time when my periods started, just prior to my thirteenth birthday. This was a monumental moment for me, not least because I had no sanitary towels at the ready. Turning to flush the toilet and seeing the blood was really scary for me. Once again I told myself if I was back in England this wouldn't be such a worry. I was resentful and felt guilty for feeling like that. I told Mum. She was great about it, putting her arms around me and giving me a hug. It was a normal part of growing up, she said. I also knew it meant I could become pregnant if he got to me. Perhaps being in a foreign country was not such a bad thing at that time after all.

I worried about school and the thought of starting at one with a minimal knowledge of a very difficult language. Grammar was particularly challenging. Sat on a park bench with Mum one day I asked about school. Unbeknown to me she had telephoned Miss Shepard at the grammar school. She had agreed to keep my place open at the school for an indefinite period of time. She never mentioned starting at a local school.

Mum had a strained relationship with her sister and brother-in-law. There was history there. After having John, Mum had pulled herself up by the bootstraps, put her head down and finally secured a clerical job at the Toronto Star newspaper in Canada. I admired her tenacity and determination. She conquered real adversity. Life was improving for both of them in Canada. They had a good life with a sustainable existence but this too was to change.

My aunt and uncle had a turbulent relationship. Their relationship, I suspected, mirrored my own parents. It was 1960. John was at school and Mum had a job when a letter arrived from my aunt pleading for her to come back to Germany as the situation with Werner was escalating. Ironically she had left Germany because Eva had kicked her out of the house they shared with Werner. Now she was asking her to return six years later to a similar set-up to the one she had left all those years before. Family ties and responsibilities won. Weeks later, back in Germany, having given up everything, she and John were now living with Eva and Werner. It didn't take long for Mum to realise the mistake she had made. This was not only the ultimate sacrifice it was also the biggest mistake she made by her own volition. Arguments ensued. Violence became common place and Mum and John were getting caught up in the constant cross fire.

She had in the preceding months struck up a friendship with a UK divorcee, Harold Yates, a school caretaker living in Salford. Perhaps he was a port in a storm. I know little of their courtship and I've no wish to second guess but within eighteen months she had arrived in the UK with John and began their life in Salford with him.

But back to Germany. A letter from the Benefits Agency dropped through the door stating we were not eligible for benefits at that time. It was a huge blow to us. Mum appealed. As in the UK there was a wait for an appeal to be heard. It could take weeks. We couldn't wait as money was rapidly running out. John's job had now finished too. We were facing a no-win situation.

I do not to this day understand why my aunt did not help us financially. After everything my mum had given up all those years before to be by her side and offer her support. Perhaps she was too proud to ask, or just too stubborn.

Four weeks later we were back where we started, undertaking a moonlight escape with rent owing and an arduous return trip to look forward to. It was dark. It was late. We left taking what we had arrived with, almost, and like all other decisions I was told what was happening. My opinion was never sought. I didn't count.

On our return we stayed at a dire bedsit in the Cheetham Hill district of Manchester. Just one room with a kitchenette, a double and single bed, a tired shabby sofa and little else. It was truly oppressive and totally unsuitable for three people. The landlord was sleazy. He was a small, slight man, no more than 5ft 8in tall with slits for eyes. He would stare at me. He reminded me of him. But, it was where we laid our heads for what turned out to be nearly a year. On the plus side we never went back to him again. Hallelujah! At last I could breathe.

As September approached school loomed. Miss Shepard had said I could return but I just couldn't. A mixture of embarrassment, fear of not being able to catch up and the constant 'Where have you been?' line of questioning prevented me. My head felt like a pressure cooker of emotion with all my fears rising rapidly to the top.

"I'm not going back," I said. "I will go to another school," I added.

Hope Park School for Girls was in the heart of the Jewish community in Prestwich. It wasn't just Jewish girls that went there though. It was deemed a good school. A respectable school in an affluent area and only fifteen minutes away. I needed a fresh start. I wanted to draw a line under the past so I could embrace the future. I knew a girl who went to the school, which was a positive start.

The teachers were for the most part friendly. Monsieur

Duprez was the French teacher. He made all the other girls go weak at the knees and his accent was soothing. Then there was Mr Goodwin. A 6ft 3in, slim maths teacher whose voice was deep and very loud. He scared me but I admired him too. During my first class with him he made a point of telling my classmates I came from 'the big school down the road', which did nothing to assist me in the popularity stakes. I suppose they thought I would behave differently. I didn't. I just wanted to fit in. To be liked for being me – Audrey.

Mrs Kay, Hope Park's very own Elsie Tanner, was the eccentric arts teacher. She was the image of Coronation Street's favourite resident with her beehive hairdo and statement earrings. I take that back, she was a cross between Bet Lynch and Elsie Tanner. Her favourite word was 'woopsy', which she used a lot in the event of arts materials being spilt or desecrated by some wayward, bored pupil. Art was a favourite subject for me, as was English Language and English Literature. The number of still life projects I undertook was seriously mind blowing. Shoes and handbags, bowls of fruit and whatever else could be found in the art room or elsewhere made up the weekly still life compositions.

PE was not my favourite subject, especially if it involved being in the gym. I was skilled at forging my mother's excuse-me notes. No mean feat if you had seen her signature. Miss Dickson was the PE teacher. She was around 5ft 4in and a little chubby in my opinion for a teacher of fitness. I do remember she loved cats. In fact she died prematurely in her early fifties. I know that because I saw her memoriam in the local newspaper. Her family expressed a wish on her behalf for donations to a cat's charity instead of flowers.

I settled in well, making friends first with a blonde, curly-haired girl called Heather. She was slim and ultra-smart. I always remember her birthday as it was precisely a week before mine. She had a couple of friends called Bev and Ruth. Bev was a quiet, tall, mousy girl who later became my best friend. Ruth was intelligent and a superb saver. She saved for everything and really big things at that. I was always in admiration of her for that. Then there were Gaynor and Cathy, who completed our gang. We were a good group, each bringing an enriching element to the pact. I vividly remember eating creme eggs in the sunshine laid on the grass banking which overlooked the school yard. We were in our own little world. Some of us definitely more than others!

I was a teenager. I wanted to have nice things. I knew in order to do that I would need to get a part-time job. At one point I had secured three. An evening newspaper round delivering to many of the large, spacious homes complete with lush swimming pools. I also worked at Lapidus, a renowned, busy Jewish-owned café two minutes from the bedsit in Cheetham Hill. It paid well. I worked all day Sunday and earned £14 which was good money then. I discovered the joy of salmon cutlets, chopped liver and bagels and cream cheese – yummy. I tried a Saturday job in a hairdressers, but my psoriasis flared up when shampooing clients as the products irritated my skin.

It was considered unsightly by my boss when working with the public and painfully itchy for me. Reluctantly I gave up my job. I then went to work as a mum's helper to a Mrs Yaffe. I assisted with her two schoolaged children. Life was busy and full and I had money in my pocket. Life was good. I had gained some control, which was satisfying.

I was generous too, taking my mum on the train to Blackpool when time allowed. I paid the train fare and Mum bought lunch. We would link arms and laugh at silly sights (usually people and not the place). We also developed a curiosity for the back street fortune tellers.

It was during this time that my career aspirations surfaced. I wanted to be involved in performing arts in some form or another. The Central Pier Theatre in Blackpool was a popular family theatre hosting the big show business names at the time. One night we booked to see 'The Mr & Mrs Show', hosted by its original presenter, the late Derek Batey. I loved the live show formula. I was hooked. On the next visit I was invited on stage by Derek Batey and there I experienced the stage in all its glory. I revelled in the sights and the smells. I was hooked. When I heard the applause I knew this industry was where I wanted to be.

Next day at school I showed my friends the Polaroid picture of me grinning like a Cheshire cat in my new white trouser suit holding hands with Derek Batey. I quickly contacted the stage manager – Ray Worthington – with a view to gaining occasional work experience there. He graciously obliged.

'Hello Again' came the cheery voice of Derek Batey accompanied by a warm hug. He was helpful and offered sound advice about working in show business. A few years later after college he invited me to Border Television in Carlisle, where he was the Assistant Controller of Programmes. He gave time out of his busy schedule to offer advice and support to me. I respected him for that. Not many celebrities would have given their time like that.

We had been in our cramped bedsit for far too long when a woman called Julia visited us. She was from Collingwood Housing Association, where our names had been added to the waiting list for a brand new apartment in Bury at a development called Berkshire Court, which adjoined the famous Bury Football Club. I recall the relief and gratitude when we were offered a tenancy. Travel to school would take a little longer but the reward of a permanent home and somewhere to finally anchor our roots was worth it.

Berkshire Court was a happy place for me. It was a lovely development of three two-storey apartments in a beautifully landscaped area. We were to be in the first block. Everything was brand new, smart and shiny. The first new possession we had ever owned. It felt like ours but it was rented. Who needed the Ritz? We had it all here. After fifteen years of upheaval and sadness maybe now at last life would take a turn for the better.

With Derek Batey 1977

With friends, outside Buckingham Palace 1978

CHAPTER THREE

NEW AND OLD

We were settling in nicely. The flat was beginning to feel like home. It was new and fresh. This was the start we all needed. There was one demon I had to face though – my father, Harold Yates, who was now living in the centre of Salford in a low-rise 1960s maisonette. I was fourteen years old and gaining in confidence, impatient and forthright with an emerging voice and a significant distrust of strangers. I was apprehensive about visiting him, having had no contact since before the 'Great Escape'. I had not seen him for more than two years by this point. This was to be the final parting as far as I was concerned. As I arrived and began walking towards his house on Sorbus Close I experienced flashbacks to the time when I was that powerless little girl. A lot had changed. I had changed, but the smells, tastes and sounds of the past reverberated within me. It was as though my internal foundations were experiencing a mini earth tremor. I knocked firmly and with deliberate intent. I didn't want to give the impression of appearing weak. He answered almost immediately. It was as though there was urgency there on his part and perhaps a desire. He greeted me with a smile and a 'Hello'. My stomach was churning as I stepped into his home.

25

If he tried anything I would kill him with the first available implement I could find and as we spent much of the time in his kitchen that would not have been difficult.

He appeared really pleased to see me. He was pathetic. I peered around cautiously. It was a regular home. Clean and tidy though somewhat understated. He had prepared some food. A cheese and onion soup, ham sandwiches arranged carefully on a china plate and some small fancy cakes fresh from the bakery it would appear. As he slowly stirred the cheese soup in the saucepan chatting away I recalled the day I fainted through lack of food. He then had no problem with solely feasting on an array of food. It was a bit like the array on offer today. I was small, scared, vulnerable and very hungry and my reward was systematic abuse. I hated him. I hated everything he represented but more than anything I hated the fact that this monster was my biological father.

He appeared kind and attentive today. He was on his best behaviour. He played the host with the most and didn't raise his voice, hand or anything else. Personally, I think he was surprised I had become an assertive, opinionated young woman. I was also as tall as him now. He seemed unsure of me, which was a first. Polite conversation gradually turned to a more direct conversation on my part. Looking back I was baiting him. It was certainly foolhardy but that small feeling of power over him was exhilarating. The memory of what was said has gone but what I do remember is eventually walking out of his front door then turning back and shouting 'you will

NEVER see me again' and he never did. What a sad, lonely, pathetic shadow he cast. If only I could have seen that as the sad little girl aged seven. If only I had found my voice to shout 'I'm being abused' when sat in Dr Solomon's office or been able to tell Mum face-to-face – or indeed had the courage to. That question to her would not be posed for another fifteen years. I felt empowered as I walked away. When I got back home I knew that man had gone from my life.

I had finished that particular episode. To know I would never have to see him again was such a relief. I discovered that terminating a relationship gave me an instant sense of relief and control which I later discovered can also unwittingly cause an awful lot of hurt to the people who came into my life.

If I wasn't me I wouldn't have anything to do with me. I'm a maelstrom of conflicting and confusing emotion. I yell at people. I labour the point too often. I get worked up over trivial matters and men don't stay around long because of it. This is the legacy of abuse which I hoped I had finally left behind.

I looked up to John. He was the brother I idolised. I didn't see the 'half'. He was in every way my brother. The three of us were a team. John was great in the kitchen. Our European heritage was constantly evident no more so than in the kitchen. The coffee percolator was on 24/7. The smell wafted through the apartment like a reassuring comfort blanket, wrapping us up and tucking us in.

The local Bury delicatessen Katsouris was a popular haunt. When John was paid he would call in and stock up on the continental creamy meat salad, soft rye bread and fresh coffee. Thursdays were our day for this. It was also the day John would supplement my earnings. I liked Thursdays.

Mum was still working at John Myers, undertaking translation work on a more regular basis. She was happier these days. She had also started dating a businessman – Charles. He was a senior executive for GEC whom she saw every morning whilst she waited for the bus to work. They went out on day trips to Harrogate or out for a drink periodically, or would catch a concert with the famous Halle Orchestra. He was kind. That was a novelty. I was happy that she was happy. John was now working as a general operative at Borden Chemicals in Bury, often bringing home gluten-free fruit cake and chocolate biscuits which, frankly, were simply awful.

One night when mum and Charles went out I planned to do nothing more than watch TV. What happened next was unexpected and once again completely destroyed my self confidence. A man just a few years older than me who was very close to our family came in. I can't remember the exact chain of events, but I found myself without my bottom halves on laid on the dark brown living room carpet while he stood over me, wrapping his penis in industrial blue cling film-type material in the absence of protection. Next thing I remember was his penis penetrating me.

Whilst this may shock you, it was not an unpleasant experience but I knew it was most definitely wrong. As his back arched he let out a gasp as he came inside me. His body was like a rag doll on top of me for a moment. Then he carefully withdrew and went to the bathroom. I lay there for a moment. It actually began to feel as though abuse was now the norm for me, that no matter how close the person was to the family I could not trust them. One thing was for sure, whether I realised it or not my relationship with this person had changed forever. I got up and slipped my knickers on, then put my jeans back on and almost carried on as though what just happened hadn't happened. It was a surreal moment and once again I was indeed on the outside looking in.

Picture for a moment a room with a large, re-enforced glass window. You see yourself about to be raped. You bang on the window with any implement at your possession but no matter how much you bang on that window the young woman cannot hear you. You are forced to watch helplessly as the tears stream down your face. You attempt to wipe them away but they just keep reappearing.

Having felt empowered following my parting from my father I had now gone right back to the beginning. From the highs of having finally beaten the man who had sexually abused me for seven long years I was back to being the little girl being used by someone I should have been able to depend on. I was beginning to think I would never be able to find a male I could truly trust. How would that affect my future? Would I ever be able to form relationships, work with men or marry or trust one enough to take the step of starting a family? On that evening a piece of me was lost forever.

My friends were there for me. They were my sanity. Bev, Ruth, Heather, Cathy and Gaynor. They were my rocks. I needed them more than ever as I now had the burden of another secret to keep.

The school careers officer was due a visit as college loomed and my year-end exams were imminent. She was a curly haired, slim female in her late thirties, I guessed typical of females in 1979. "What would you like to do?" She asked.

"I want to be in show business," I replied.

"Hmm," she said, thumbing through her paperwork before handing me a print out on of all things – a secretarial course!

I sat incredulous. The woman was going through options which were clearly very stereotypical of the era. I knew at that moment that my career path was my responsibility. I was keen as mustard. Proactive with a terrier-like instinct. Nothing would stop me!

Salford College came to my attention. I had heard they ran a two-year foundation course in drama and theatre. I could learn to act and understand the theory side, too. OK, that wasn't as attractive but hey, you can't have everything. My interview was with a middle aged, slim man called Roland. He was the dishevelled course leader. A bit like the Michael Caine character from *'Educating Rita'*. He sported the typical tutor apparel of corduroy jacket with well-worn elbow patches. I remember nothing of my audition interview apart from being terrified. A few days later a letter popped through the letter box. I had passed the audition and could start the course at the beginning of September 1979. I was exhilarated and terrified all rolled into one. I had done it and more importantly I had done it by myself. I was a woman on a mission. I focussed on the task in hand and wasn't distracted by negative people like the careers officer.

Salford College on Peru Street was a crumbling building with an institution-type quality about it akin to the performing arts school in the TV series 'Fame'. It had its fair share of colourful characters. Gordon the portly, bearded acting coach with a bellow to match his belly was the quintessential head of acting. He was a true task master in every sense of the word. He did nothing for my confidence. He terrified me like Mr Goodwin at Hope Park had – but at least I liked him!

A few weeks in, during an acting class, he asked me to scream. Not once, not twice but several times. I was holding myself back. I wasn't fully giving myself, he said. I was now hot, red in the face and hoarse. I wasn't sure this acting shenanigan was for me. My fellow students all seemed so much more proficient at it than me. I shared classes with Ayub Khan Din, who went on to create 'East is East', and Nick Conway, the lovable 'Billy Boswell' from 'Bread', not forgetting Christopher Ecclestone of 'Doctor Who' fame from the year above!

Once again, I didn't really feel as though I fitted in and neither did Marc, with whom I struck up a friendship. He looked very much like a curly-haired version of Rowan Atkinson. He was olive skinned, medium height, quiet for an acting student but highly intelligent. His dad was a solicitor and his mum was an actor often working on 'Coronation Street'. They welcomed me into their family, recognising the positive effect I appeared to have on their son. I was quite often a dinner guest at their beautiful detached home in Gatley, Cheshire. Maureen's French Onion soup was to die for!

Marc was only ever a friend. No more than that but we gelled well and we did have a fair few laughs. Marc's grandmother Gladys lived very close to the college by Irlam o' th' Heights. She would bring us a tray each with a steaming bowl of tomato soup complete with lots of fresh buttered bread. It was heaven and she was lovely. Gladys was the grandma I never had the pleasure of knowing.

I noticed Marc ate his food very slowly and carefully. I always finished mine way before him. I asked him why once. He told me he had a fear of choking. We became partners in crime but both knew that the course wasn't for us, so we sought an alternative.

Marc's mum had offered to take the lease out on a corner shop

Marc had viewed in Flixton Manchester owned by Mr and Mrs Challiner, a retired couple. Mr Challiiner was a Mason. Marc suggested I run the shop with him. I said 'yes' without too much thought. My mum didn't seem to mind either. I knew his parents would cushion our initial months in the business. Marc had just passed his test and his parents had bought him a car so trips to the Cash & Carry would not be a problem. I was nearly seventeen and running a shop with no experience. It was challenging and we fell out a million times. On my seventeenth birthday he took me for a lunchtime drink at the local pub. I was never a drinker and it didn't take much to make me drunk, so the seven Special Brew lagers he bought me were definitely going to have an effect on me.

Back at the shop I was slumped at the bottom of the stairs that led to the Challiner's private quarters. I felt like I was dying. Marc didn't know what to do and the Challiners were less than impressed, calling my mum to come and collect me, which was much worse I thought. I tried to sober up. I'll never forget the look of shame on my mother's face. She was so apologetic to the Challiners and I never lived it down. On the plus side I never got that drunk ever again.

A few short months later I quit the shop, but we remained friends. Marc quit soon after. But I was left with no path to follow. I had quit college. I had quit the shop. Queue my next adventure. One which was to take me six thousand miles away to Chicago!

CHAPTER FOUR

THE MID-WEST

One night I was thumbing through the Manchester Evening News when an advertisement caught my eye. A Chicago family were looking for a mother's help for their three children, aged twelve, eight and two. Was this the new adventure I needed? Could I push my boundaries and go to what to me was the other side of the world? I put the newspaper down and went off momentarily, but later came back to it. My curiosity and 'what if?' mentality was taking over. I studied the advertisement in more detail. Please write to Mrs Jelinek stating why you would like to live with our family. I would do just that.

I'd done nothing apart from lounge around since leaving the shop. I was so bored. I was now eighteen and a half. Time to explore new vistas, I thought, so I penned my letter, remembering to tell them about my time as a mother's help to Mrs Yaffe and her children. Outwardly I was confident. I had learned to craft that illusion and occasionally I actually believed it. Inwardly I constantly fought my many demons. My internal dialogue was exceedingly loud and aggressive at times.

I was becoming used to scaring myself rigid and then doing it anyway, so pen to paper I wrote my letter to Mrs Jelinek and pretty much put it to the back of my mind. One Sunday afternoon just into January 1981, four months after I first applied, the telephone rang. Mum answered it. "It's for you. An American woman," she whispered. I was confused. Actually I thought it was a prank. "Hi Audrey. It's your American family here," she joked. "Sorry for the delay in replying. We would like to offer you the job," she said chirpily. I didn't know how to answer. Once again my emotions were on full cycle. I was given a week to make up my mind before the return call would come and I would have to give my answer.

It was a hell of a week. My mum understandably was anxious. She took the realist viewpoint. What would happen if something went wrong? It was too far to just come over and bail me out if the dream went sour and it would be way too costly. But just as she saw the negatives I was seeing the positives. Tall buildings, yellow cabs and dinners with cute guys like I had seen on the movies. Reality of course can be a very different matter. I started the month in our cosy Berkshire Court abode and would finish it in a very snowy suburb of Chicago called Northbrook. True to form on the 24th January 1981 I set off to Heathrow by coach on my own. After checking in I rang mum. "You can come home. You don't have to go," she said. "But I want to," and that was that.

As the plane came in to land early evening at O'Hare

International Airport I was surprised by the amount of tall skyscrapers immediately surrounding the airport. I was so excited. Mr Jelinek was to meet me as I came through immigration, if I got through immigration.

Nowadays there is an official programme for au pairs and nannies wishing to work overseas. It's properly regulated to protect the interests of the family and the worker. Hours are set. Wages are fair and there is an independent body to talk to in the event of dispute. Back in 1981 there was little to speak of and many girls entered the US illegally in effect. Strangely, I never thought I was doing anything illegal. I was offered the chance to experience a life overseas for up to a year. That was it. Naïve I know but my wanderlust was strong. I had the chance a lot of my friends would have died for. I wasn't about to give it up without a fight.

I did feel a little nervous as I got to the immigration queue. Everything was bigger than back at home. It was like seeing everything magnified many, many times over.

The sights and the smells were all alien to me. My tummy was doing somersaults worthy of an Olympic event. My host family had mailed me the airline ticket, which was one way. After a satisfactory duration of stay they would pay my return fare. I did feel anxious about this. I also had very little money on me. Thirty pounds to be exact. In my single suitcase alongside my winter weight clothes was a photo of two of my charges, Michael aged eleven, Jamie aged eight and Danny aged two. The picture displayed the two older kids on a summer vacation wearing stetson-type hats.

I was called to the desk by an officious-looking guy in his early thirties wearing a pale blue shirt and navy trousers. I tentatively handed him my passport. He stared at the image, then me, then at the image again. There was no emotion there, just a blank, motionless stare. It was truly disconcerting.

"How long you staying for?" he said.

"A couple of weeks," I'd been told to say.

"Where are you staying?" he said, examining my passport.

"With family friends," I replied.

It was important to answer confidently even if I felt less than confident. See my time doing drama may be about to pay off!

"How much money do you have with you?" he enquired.

I must have looked a little panicked as I knew I only had about thirty pounds on me and nothing else. If they asked to see what I had on me that would probably have been that followed by a swift deportation back to the UK. I noticed there was no one else from my flight in any of the queues, just me.

The next thing I knew I was being asked to step into an office. Now I was worried. The neon strip light was causing havoc with my tired, bleary eyes but the 6ft 7in, skinny, red-headed guy stood behind his desk with my suitcase open in front of him didn't help. I remember seeing the picture of the children which was now on top of the clothing instead of tucked within where it had previously been. I knew I needed to answer all questions confidently and calmly if I was to have any chance of being allowed into this windy, cold city.

Stood on the other side of the desk I was asked pretty much the same questions as the officer before him. The only difference being he had a far more probing manner and was really interested to know why I had such a small amount of money with me. I told him I was a guest and wouldn't need anything as it was their treat as family friends. He asked questions about the family and the picture of the kids but I just kept giving him the answers I figured he wanted.

An hour into this and so tired I could hardly stand up I piped up: "I am a guest in your country and would like to be treated as such. I am here on holiday for two weeks visiting friends. That's it. So please, either let me in or send me home." I know calling someone's bluff is a dangerous tactic but I'd had enough.

He paused for a moment, dropped the lid on my suitcase then looked me in the eye and said: "OK. I am going to grant you entry into the United States but if I find out you are here for any other reason than a vacation I'll personally make sure this is the last vacation you ever take." And with that he said, "Welcome to Chicago," leaving me to repack my suitcase. My legs were like jelly. My mouth was dry and my heart was racing but I had done it. I was officially in The Windy City! As I entered the Arrivals Hall I had no idea if Randy (Mr Jelinek) would even still be there. Thankfully he was. Smiling with relief he called out my name. Randy was a mid-thirties, curly-haired, big guy. His smiley face put me at ease. I just wanted to get the hell out of there. As we stepped out into the bitter Chicago night my three-quarter-length cowboy boots were woefully inadequate; the snow seeped above the leather rims wetting my legs instantly.

Northbrook was an affluent suburb of Chicago twenty minutes from the city. Quail Lane had a mixture of homely, large, detached family properties alongside the odd palatial, white-pillared property. It was so pretty covered in snow and their home was very much a family home rather than a show home. As we stepped from the car the elder two children excitedly greeted me, staying up way past their bedtime I suspect. I hit it off instantly with Michael, who was a mature, intelligent, good-looking boy with a love of music, sport and magic.

Jamie held my hand and led me into their home where their mum was. Mrs J was your typical glamorous housewife but in casual clothing. She was very slim and very attractive. I felt wholly inadequate in her company. My first memory there was being sat at the kitchen table showing Michael a card trick, which he thought was really cool. I had made an impression. Tired out I headed for my room and a well-earned rest before my work began the next day.

Before I left for Chicago I was given the number for Theresa, a Liverpool girl three years older than me who was a nanny for the Jelinek's best friends, Al and Sue.

Al was an attorney in the City. Their home was very much a show home. I always felt uncomfortable when I visited. Theresa was fantastic and we hit it off almost immediately. She was a great support and her age gave her the wisdom I lacked but needed. Al and Sue had a tempestuous relationship, often arguing in front of us or in an adjoining room whereas my family didn't – well not in my earshot anyway.

One of the first things I did was to go to the local store and buy an album for Michael, whose birthday fell during those first few days I was there. It was an album by the British band The Police. I was as thrilled to buy it for him almost as much as he was to receive it. He looked genuinely surprised and Mrs J chastised me for spending it on him but he was a great kid so why not? Those first few days were enlightening, fun, and delightful, despite the horrible jet lag I was experiencing.

Mrs J had a long list of chores and instructions for me which were added to weekly. I worked six days a week with one day off – Sunday, which gave me a chance to meet up with the other English girls and hang out. There were about six of us with me being the youngest. I think they took me under their wing, particularly as the novelty of being in America began to wear off. Work kicked in and so did the homesickness after about five weeks. I missed Mum and John more than I ever expected. It was tough.

During the day toddler Danny was my priority and boy did he make me work. He was like an untamed animal. Clearly treated like the baby in every way being afforded every excuse possible for his behaviour, which was fine when mom was in charge but not when I had him. He was a strong-willed child. If he didn't want to do something he would scream the house down if you tried to get him to do it. He had a fascination for any room that wasn't his, causing havoc. He particularly liked my room, which was kind of cool with its black-and-white lines and touches of colour, modern furniture and a fresh, young feel.

Mrs J wanted me to get Danny into the shorts she had bought him for the warmer days to come. There was a drawer full of them but he wasn't having any of it. I tried to reason with him. Make a joke of it but nothing would work. Then I discovered bribery. Give him a forbidden sugary snack and I could coax him into a pair for short periods at a time. He wasn't stupid was he? The longer it took the more forbidden snacks he was given and the more hyper he became. But after less than ten days it was mission accomplished and as his mom came home one afternoon he was wearing his new shorts without argument. Mrs J was over the moon and promptly rewarded him with said sugary snack, unaware he had been eating them for days. I too went up in her estimation, albeit temporarily.

The British girls wanted a night out at Brannigans, a Chicago night spot. Great for them as twenty-one and overs but not so good for me as the baby of the group. I was worried. I didn't want to be refused entry but they were my friends and I wanted to go. None of us earned much and taxis were expensive, so we would always pool our money making sure we kept enough back for the fare home. I kept reciting my new date of birth until it became second nature. The girls paraded up the dimly lit steps to the club without question. I tried to follow swiftly behind but felt this hand on my shoulder and the "how old are you and when were you born" routine. I was becoming adept at getting myself out of sticky situations. After all, I got through interrogation at O'Hare International. I needn't have worried. Before long the alcohol was gushing through our veins. Now I know I said earlier I never got drunk again after the Special Brew saga, but I did just about remember how to get merry.

The night was long and our memory was short when it came to keeping enough money back for the cab home. We were up the creek without a paddle. Our only course of action was to book a cab and pretend to have lost our purse on reaching our destination. Trust us then to get a clued up cabby who enquired half-way to our destination about our ability to pay, leading to us being threatened with the police and being kicked out of the cab in darkness and in unfamiliar surroundings. We had no choice but to contact one of our families for help – and guess who drew the short straw?

You can probably deduce the dressing down I was given on my return. "Irresponsible" was the buzz word for several days as was: "What would your mom say?" I realised being the youngest of the nannies was not always an advantage!

The weeks went by and as they did my homesickness took a real grip. I missed my mum and John and life back in the UK. I had also begun putting on lots of weight. I was comfort eating. The food was loaded with calories which my body appeared to be storing vociferously. My size 10/12 days were fast becoming a dim and distant memory.

During one of my weepy telephone calls to the UK John asked if I wanted to come home. The months had been tough and my relationship with Mrs J was constantly strained. In a heartbeat I said "yes". I knew I would have to find the air fare home myself as the family would only pay my return fare if I stayed a full year. It was vitally important I kept my plan a secret from the family. I had to carry on as normal, whatever that meant.

This was feeling like another great escape in the making. As I came back down the stairs from my room I sensed an atmosphere. I walked a little nervously towards the laundry room to finish folding the children's clothes. Mr J appeared at the doorway to the laundry room with Mrs J in tow. I sensed a storm was brewing and pretty quickly at that. "We heard you," she said frostily. Don't panic girl I thought. "Your conversation to your family?" They had the speaker on. They were listening. That's nice I thought. What happened to privacy? They made out it was accidently on speaker phone. Yeah, right of course it was. My heart was in my mouth and my pulse was racing. I looked and felt guilty.

The chat that followed was strained. It was very much two against one. Clearly they thought I had been reasonably happy. I tried to explain the homesickness was occupying my every waking moment and that it wasn't fair on me or the children. Eventually they left me to it but I knew they weren't going to make it easy for me to leave. Well, she wouldn't anyway.

They pretty much ignored me from that moment on, other than to deliver work-related commands. Looking back they were unreasonable. I was eighteen years old working a million hours a week for £30 in a strange country with no family around me.

The next four weeks in the lead up to my departure felt like a year. I continued to make arrangements for my return. John was struggling to get the fare home together but he promised me he would find it. Then they pulled the rug from under me. They wanted the air fare they had paid for me to come out back. What? Now they were being unreasonable. I had stayed half my time and worked hard. Then came the threat. If we don't get the money back we will report you to the authorities. Had I stepped back for a moment and thought about it I would have realised that they would have been in just as much trouble for employing me but I was frightened. I thought I was trapped there. An American nanny friend, Terri, had spoken to her family. Their friends needed a nanny. They offered to come and collect me and take me to their home. It was kind, very kind but I wondered if I might be going from bad to worse and anyway the homesickness was very much still there. John called a few days later after finding out and spoke to my family. It turned out he was selling his beloved motorbike to pay the extra money needed. I felt awful. My family had no money to spare whereas Mr Jelinek ran a catalogue store, Oak Supply. It employed twenty-plus staff and provided a very comfortable lifestyle. They didn't need the money.

Four weeks later I left. I was sad at leaving the children but more sad at leaving alone. No one said goodbye, thanks or anything else for that matter. They were all shut in one room deliberately. I shut the door behind me and left with a lift from Terri to the airport. My American dream had ended.

The Jelineks with Danny aged 2

CHAPTER FIVE

REDCOATS!

Now twenty years old my show business passions had reared their head again and so had my confidence. If ever the time was right to pursue a career it was now. I had stumbled across a recruitment notice for Butlins Redcoats. I knew the likes of Shane Ritchie and Des O'Connor had cut their teeth as a Redcoat and they hadn't done too badly, so I applied.

After a few days I received a letter from a gentleman called Joe Cousins inviting me to an interview at Fountain Street Job Centre, Manchester. Nervous but excited I was greeted by him with a firm, friendly handshake and a smile. I felt immediately at ease, which no doubt helped me through this particular interview process.

As I was ushered to my seat I expected to be asked to do singing cartwheels or fire eating at the very least, so I was a little surprised and relieved to be asked: "Just tell me about yourself." So I did. My conversational ease sat well with Joe, who was the Entertainments Manager for the Skegness Complex. It didn't feel like an interview. It was more like an informal chat with the desk between us as the only clue that this was an interview setting.

Butlins is a British entertainment institution attracting at that time (1984) ten thousand holiday makers a week at the height of the season. I knew there was kudos to wearing a red jacket. This would be a steep learning curve but a fantastic opportunity none the less.

There were around twenty redcoats being sought. Redcoats were to start early May. It was now March. That's good, I thought. Then he told me that the year before they had eight thousand applications to be Redcoats. My heart sank. My opportunity had just developed wings and was slowly flying into the distance and out of sight. As the days passed I almost forgot about the job, resigning myself to the reality that I probably would not get a positive response back anyway. The odds were just too high.

My mum was housekeeping for a Jewish family in Whitefield, an affluent suburb of North Manchester. They had two young children, Louisa and Daniel. Mum had volunteered me to look after the children on a few afternoons whilst their mum was occupied with other things. It was a pretty easy job. They were well behaved. Louisa was a diabetic. I was in awe of the fact that a young child injected herself twice a day without a second thought. Daniel loved his toy vacuum cleaner and Phillips Park was close by. It was extra money for me. I was in between jobs so it became a welcome income. I had given Butlins the family number in case they needed to contact me. As the children occupied themselves with their pens, drawing paper and assorted arts materials the telephone rang. It was Joe Cousins. After a brief chit chat I was told I was now officially on standby to go to Butlins. To say I was surprised and pleased was an understatement.

So now there was a real prospect of going and I really wanted it. My God, I would be crushed if it failed to materialise now. After a few nerve wracking days I received the confirmation I so very much wanted. I would indeed become a Butlins Redcoat.

When I arrived a week before the season started I remember thinking this looks like an army camp, everything from the checkpoint entry through to the 'hut'-style buildings where I was to collect my uniform. Perhaps I had signed up for years and not months and no one had told me. I would love to tell you my uniform was new and crisp but the reality was that this was someone else's. The jacket disappointed. It was tired looking, made from a kind of polyester-type material with buttons that had become a little too stretched by someone's girth in the past. I was to be a General Duty Redcoat. We were the backbone of the entertainment department. If there was an event or activity we ran it or supported it. Our induction week soon showed which fellow Redcoats you would enjoy working alongside and the ego-busting ones you wouldn't! Clearly it would be wrong to name anyone here so I won't – tempted though I am.

As the season commenced I hit the ground running. I spent my days from eight am until midnight Monday to Saturday bending over backwards to keep the guests happy. I signed lots of autographs and posed for lots and lots of photographs. Guests quite often forgot we were mere 'coats' and would hijack us moments before our midnight finish to ask advice on plumbing issues or leaky radiators. Politely and always with a smile we would refer them to the relevant department.

We lived amongst the guests and they loved it. We ate with them too. I used to crave my bed at the end of an arduous day though. It was the treat that very soon replaced the novelty of drinks after work. The hours were long and I got through numerous pairs of white shoes during the course of the season. I sported an intermittent sore throat or infection on several occasions which made me a very croaky bingo caller but I loved it, all of it. I felt I had at last found my niche. I was at home at Butlins. My efforts had not gone unnoticed by the management either and gradually I was given the opportunity to compere and learnt how to DJ in the Empress Suite.

Butlins held a weekly Donkey Derby. Children rode the donkeys and parents could bet. Back in1984 to scoop the total winnings at the end of the week could amount to £1,400 plus. It was a popular money spinner and a huge laugh too as cantankerous animals were often assisted with a gentle shove during a race – and that was just the Redcoats! I was soon given an extra responsibility – just another to add to my ever-burgeoning list, that of a Donkey Derby ticket seller. It was gambling with a capital 'G' but with £1,400-plus weekly average prize money it was a tidy sum to win.

There was fierce competition amongst those chosen as sellers and we got commission too, which was a very welcome addition to our paltry wage. I worked hard at it and found myself to be good, achieving high weekly sales. A few weeks into the season I was called into the office. I was worried. Got to be honest I thought I was going to be given my marching orders but instead to my utter surprise I was offered the job of Chief Donkey Derby ticket seller, a role never given to a female at Skegness. Talk about girl power. I was thrilled to bits and really proud.

Time rolled by. I was settling in and making friends. I had become friendly with Dave, the resident disc jockey. He had a cheeky way about him and we got on really well. He started to teach me how to operate the decks, which was a great diversion in more ways than one. It was also an additional skill I used frequently. Dave and I were beginning to break away from the others. We were becoming a couple. We discovered a fantastic little bistro in the adjoining town of Ingoldmells. Their homemade chicken soup was heaven on earth.

A local club nearby had a little-known act called Black Lace appearing. The two boys who fronted the group had visited Dave at Butlins earlier in the week to ask if he would promote their new record '*Agadoo*'. He did. It proved popular. At the club Dave cheekily asked if they would do a spot at Butlins where they could perform the song and the accompanying dance alongside the Redcoats. When they agreed we thought they were just being polite in our presence. We had been performing it for the previous three or four weeks and knew it back to front and upside down. We never expected the boys to come until the Assistant Entertainments Manager Bill came running over to say Black Lace would be at the Centre in less than two hours! What a scoop. Dave and I were assigned to meet them at the gates. I was eating an ice cream cone at the time. One of boys cheekily snatched it from me and ate some of it. Anyone else and I would have boxed their ears. Our guests loved the impromptu visit from the boys. Hundreds of guests crammed themselves into the Empress Ballroom dancing and singing along with the boys, who soon after achieved a number one hit with the song. It was a fantastic moment for everyone.

That evening in the Empress Ballroom I performed the repertoire of novelty dances for our guests to join in with including *'Superman'* and of course *'Agadoo'*. Dave often got us all up several times a night for his own entertainment, I suspect. It was so hot in there. Company policy stipulated that your red jacket remained on at all times. I lost heaps of weight that summer I can tell you.

The end of the evening always featured a medley of Abba covers from the resident band. Tonight was special. It was the eve of my twenty-first birthday. As the final notes of *'Dancing Queen'* played and the clock struck midnight I saw a Redcoat carrying a lit birthday cake walking onto the stage followed by the other Redcoats. The band announced it was my twenty-first and I was beckoned to the centre of the stage as they sang *'Happy Birthday'*. Holiday makers, staff and my fellow 'coats joined it. It was an emotional moment for me. I was touched by the affection shown by everyone. It will forever remain in my memory as the most memorable birthday ever.

As the lights dimmed and the equipment was switched off people began trickling over towards our chalet. It was a compact property to say the least. A double bed. A rickety single MFI-type white wardrobe, occasional table, small bathroom, no kitchen and that was it. Hot drinks were made with a plug-in immersion heater. On a cold day it was a welcome piece of equipment, heating all those Pot Noodles, soups and copious amounts of coffee.

Within ten minutes people were knocking on our door – including the resident band. So many turned up that we had to employ crowd control. How popular was I? It was deemed a roaring success, though I remember little of the party. Someone had made a punch and I drank several glasses of that, rendering me completely useless very quickly!

Morning came and as I slowly opened one eye and then the other I witnessed what could only be described as 'Devastation Street'. There were bodies littered everywhere, including someone asleep on top of the wardrobe. Yes, that rickety piece of wood was supporting a human form. The black bin from outside the chalet was now inside with a person asleep on top of it. Outside the maintenance staff were deep in conversation as to the whereabouts of the heavy-duty bin. I was just drifting off when I heard a loud tapping on the door and Bill my manager shouting "Come on you lot. Wakey, wakey our guests await us."

I dragged myself out of bed, falling over someone sprawled out across the floor in the process. Following a wash, scant make-up application and the largest pair of dark glasses I could find I ventured outside. Bill shook his head with a smile and greeted me. "Don't shout," I said. "I'm not," he laughed. The day proved long and painful as I self-administered regular doses of paracetamol and black coffee, longing for the clock to strike midnight.

Midnight Cabaret was the sophisticated adult-only event at Butlins. It was ticket only and intensely popular. Top names performed, including Bob Monkhouse and Joe Longthorne. On a number of occasions we would be asked to get an autograph from a celebrity. They usually obliged. Quite often we would ask during breaks in a show. I do remember knocking on one dressing room door and being greeted by a scantily dressed celebrity. I didn't know where to look. I must admit I did blush as he signed the programme before I returned it to the very happy guest.

Dave and I were most definitely an item now. I think I thought I was in love. I must have done, because we announced our engagement there to the delight of our friends.

One very hot August morning we were told Yorkshire Television were coming to film a day at Butlins with us. I noticed a group of Redcoats in a line preparing to be interviewed by Richard Whiteley. Joe Cousins told me to go and stand at the front of them. I sensed the daggers drawn as I took my place at the head of it. As Richard introduced us all, 'Uncle Ron' the clown dressed in his colourful attire continually hit me on the head with his plastic hammer. It's hard to be taken seriously when a silly man is doing that to you but I smiled, as all of us did. It's a smile that's permanently pasted on your face for the whole of the season. The day though exciting was long, tiring and fun, and it was long remembered for weeks afterwards by new guests, who remarked on the annoying toy hammer man.

As the season finale night arrived and so the last night of the weekly Redcoat Show we just knew high jinks were to be the order of the evening, and true to form they were. The stage management team were on a hell-bent mission as microphones for tall people were now tiny. Small stools were now giant chairs and equipment was doctored as part of the fun. I played a nurse in a deliberately ill-fitting costume attending to a sick young man in bed. The scene culminated with my patient pulling me on top of him, but to get an even bigger laugh the crew decided to partially saw the legs on the bed. As my patient grabbed me the bed collapsed spectacularly with an almighty thud revealing even more of me than was already showing. The audience roared and so did the backstage crew.

Following the show in the bar I was blushing wildly as the smirks, nudges and winks came aplenty. My already memorable season certainly finished with a bang. I had arrived at Butlins a singleton but was now leaving as part of a committed pair. Was this to be a decision I would regret?

Redcoat, Skegness, 1984

CHAPTER SIX

YORKSHIRE LIFE

Mexborough in South Yorkshire was to be my destination with Dave after the season at Butlins finished in October 1984. We were going to live together in a small flat above the bicycle repair shop owned by his father. It was situated along a busy main road. The road was busy but the shop never appeared to be. His dad saw a stream of young kids come in with punctures or broken chains. He charged pennies to fix them. He was way too nice to run a business. He appeared uncomfortable when it came to making a profit from his target customers – children.

Butlins had offered us both a repeat season. I was up for it until I discovered that they wanted Dave to invest in newer, more expensive equipment in line with the refurbishment programme happening there. He just didn't feel it was viable to return so I declined the invite too, which in retrospect was a mistake. They do say look forward and not back so I sought new adventures but this time with Dave.

In early 1985 our chance came when a company called Imperial Inns and Taverns advertised for trainee public house managers. After a little coaxing and with no real work the decision was an easy one. We applied. Following a couple of nerve-racking interviews and profiling we were offered a traineeship. We were thrilled. Within six months to a year we could be running a pub of our own. How fantastic!

Our training began at the White Hart Hotel in Grantham, Lincolnshire. It was a quaint guest house run by Pete and Yvonne. They were a hardworking, straight talking Yorkshire couple. As typical of the time the boys ran the bar whilst the girls ran the kitchen. Yvonne and I worked relentlessly while Dave and Pete appeared to just prop up the bar. Our training manager was an ex-Scotland Yard detective, Ken Martin. Let's just say he knew Dave's past was less than ideal but was fair with him. "Be straight with me and I'll respect you for it," he would say. Dave – known for his waffling – became tongue tied and flustered in Ken's company. I liked Ken and there was a mutual respect.

Dave had spent time in a Young Offenders Unit following car thefts as a teenager. He had taken a car with a friend, losing control of the vehicle and ending up in a canal upside down. Fortunately both managed to escape but he paid the price with a custodial sentence. We worked hard and it didn't go unnoticed at HQ. Within six weeks we were ripped from the bosom of our adopted mum and dad and sent on our first relief for a two-week period at the Old Five Bells, Northampton. It was a baptism of fire for us. We hit the ground running. It was full of bike enthusiasts, a spit-and-sawdust place but the customers were sound. My ear drums took a battering though. The pressure on Dave and I to do a good job was immense. It felt like we almost had to prove ourselves more than any other trainee couple there to compensate for Dave's less-than-shiny background.

The tensions between us were rising and his temper was on the rise too. I tried to be the peacemaker. I made excuses for him, I know that now. We did a good job. Management gave us a pat on the back and next followed a Nottingham nightclub with pilfering issues and a landlord lockout near the Hillsborough stadium in Sheffield, before a longer relief at a pub restaurant in Raunds, Wellingbrough. This was a large though quieter, more select public house in a more affluent area.

I knew Dave came to the pub game with a spent criminal record and so did Ken. Imperial had secured a temporary Justices on Licence for the pub which would last no more than three months before having to apply for the Full Licence. As Dave had secured the temporary licence there was no reason to suspect the full licence would not be granted. We ran the pub like clockwork. We bought a dog – Tess, an Alsation cross who kept guard – and before long we felt at home and were accepted by the local stalwarts. As the day of the licence approached the tensions rose between us. It was no longer so easy to calm troubled waters with him. Tempers were frayed. One evening after closing he held me by the throat against a wall. It was frightening and upsetting. This was the man I loved. The man I would soon marry. I had suffered enough violence and abuse as a child. Surely I would not have to go through that all over again?

Simon, the area manager, had said weeks before that getting married or at least having set a date would strengthen our application for licensing, which we had set already for October 1985 some two months later. He visited the day before our application was to be heard. He was confident. In fact everyone within IIT management was.

We hadn't discussed what would happen if the licence was refused. It just didn't bear thinking about. This was our home. This was our livelihood. Everyone was on edge. Ken called to send his good wishes. He was more like a friend now. Dave went to court. I ran the pub. My thoughts were obviously elsewhere. On his return our worst fears were realised. The licence had been blocked by the police. Dave was deemed 'not a fit and proper person' to hold the licence. Our career was now in doubt as was our livelihood and the roof over our heads. We could continue as relief managers living out of a suitcase indefinitely or move back to Yorkshire. Reluctantly, we made the decision to move back. And so time passed.

Dave now had a driving job and I was training as a youth and community worker for Bury Education Department before we secured a steward-and-spouse post in Elton, Bury. I could still have applied for evening youth work when I qualified, but as it happened I was offered a trainee paid post, which was practically unheard of at that time.

Roll forward to March 1987. I was now married and eight months pregnant, and we were running Elton Conservative Club in Bury, Manchester. Beset with management problems and a rat infestation we moved into our first home on Ainsworth Road, Radcliffe, which was far from ready for our new family but was our only option. The family pooled their talents and resources to get the house in a liveable state for the arrival of Gemma, born on 14 April 1987 at Fairfield General Hospital, Bury. She was the apple of our eye. A bright little button with a curiosity to match, followed by Josh five years later after an early miscarriage in between. This was very early on in the pregnancy and was the most excruciating experience. Despite intense pain I would not go to the hospital. After three hours of gripping my stomach for dear life I went to the toilet and felt it drop. I couldn't look. This was my way of dealing with it. I think about that child often and what might have been.

I was now working as a youth worker and my mum was my child minder until her health took a turn for the worse. Relations between Dave and I had become worse. Arguments became the norm. Dave never knew I had been abused as a teen. It came out one day during an argument. Instead of being offered his understanding and love I was greeted with blame. Blame for not telling him sooner and letting the abuser and his wife look after our kids. It was at this time I also fell out big time with my half-brother. I screamed at John not to contact me again – and worse still

Mum took John's side not mine. It was at that point I realised what I already knew all along. She favoured John over me. I recall her saying once: "You can be just like your father." That hurt.

What about me? What about my relationship? I was depressed. I fought my demons daily. I loathed and hated myself. This was my fault. I should have been a more loveable child and then the abuse would not have happened. I felt so alone. There didn't seem to be anyone I could confide in, which became a pattern. I had carried this heavy weight around for most of my life. Aged thirty, I met Mum for lunch and for the first time in my adult life I asked her if she knew about the abuse inflicted on me by my father. "I had an idea," she said and that was that. What? No: "I'm sorry. I let you down. Forgive me." Just those four words. It was a case of placing a big thick line under those years. Forget about it. If only it was so easy for me to forget. That was to be the last time I saw Mum or John. Though John did try and call me. It was to tell me Mum was unwell, but I screamed at him down the telephone and I slammed it down on him mid conversation without finding out my beloved Mum was indeed gravely ill.

Time had moved on. I was now working for Salford City Council as an Arts Project Officer working many more hours than was necessary to avoid going home to face Dave and the awful atmosphere.

One night, following another of Dave's hands around the

throat and threat of a slapping, I decided enough was enough. My nerves were shattered. If it had not been for the children I would have taken some tablets to make the whole bloody mess go away, but they needed me.

As we went to bed I was aware of my own breathing which was rapid and shallow. I could not carry on like this. Gemma was nine and Josh was four. Both were dropped off at their school in the morning and I went on to work. As I arrived and sat in my office my colleague Renee arrived and I broke down in tears. I had cried many times before but this was different. These were tears I could not stop. Renee suggested I call Alan. He was my boss and mentor at Bury and had become a great support. He was also the Head of Educational Welfare for Bury. As colleagues Chris, my manager, and I waited nervously to hear how his surgery had gone. Alan had undergone an amputation of a leg a few years before. There was closeness between the three of us at that time, he was probably my one true friend. I could hardly see the buttons as I dialled. I was incoherent. Alan, bless him, came straight away. He knew what Dave was like.

As he arrived I broke down. I told Alan how bad his violence towards me had become. Ironic really as I was working in a deprived area regularly facing angry young men where I put myself in danger on more than one occasion. As the emotion poured out from me Alan made a call to the Domestic Crime Unit in Bury. At that moment my life was to change forever.

That evening the children and I would be spending our first evening in a Manchester refuge. It was just days before Christmas. What the hell had happened? I had failed myself and my children. As my mum was now dead, the refuge was to become our home for the next ten weeks.

CHAPTER SEVEN

FORCED BEGINNINGS

February 1997 saw us being offered a three-bedroom council property in Salford. It was on a flagship estate which was quiet and safe for the children. Josh explored his surroundings and made friends quickly. After ten traumatic weeks in the refuge it truly was an enormous relief to be able to make a fresh start in a new home as a threesome.

After a few months I felt ready to socialise. I discovered a dating column in the local newspaper. It appeared to have a number of professionals advertising to find love and friendship. After studying the column for a few nights I took the plunge and placed an advertisement of my own. I left it for a week and then checked my inbox. I had mail! One reply in particular stood out. It was from a divorced doctor called Peter. He was looking for love but was happy to make some friends along the way. He liked my profile and volunteered a contact number if I wished to get in touch. There was no pressure and it felt right so a few days later I did indeed make contact.

Our first meeting was nerve wracking but fun. As we sat having a drink he immediately put me at my ease. The time rolled by and before long our evening together had come to an end. As we parted company he expressed a wish to meet me again. He was considerably older than me. He was calm and controlled. His presence had a soothing effect on me and I did want to meet him again.

I quickly realised his work came first. I found it interesting when he talked about it. He was a maxillo facial surgeon. In a nutshell he fixed damage to the face below the nose. Dog bites and car accident injuries were commonplace for him. He was a highly skilled professional. At first I was in awe of him, until his work begun to get in the way of our time together. Calls cancelling arrangements made were disappointing and frustrating in equal measures.

When we were together he often seemed preoccupied. Peter had been married before and had come out of a relationship and had a twelve-year-old son. He had a strained relationship with his ex-wife. I didn't delve too deeply, instead letting him volunteer information when he saw fit. I quickly developed feelings for him. He was welcomed into our home. We had some wonderful evenings together, but the continual arranging and rearranging of our dates was beginning to get to me. I needed continuity. I needed to feel safe and secure. I wanted to be the centre of his world sometimes.

I tried to bite my tongue and hide my disappointment but invariably my resentment resulted in an argument. I snapped once telling him that was it. I didn't mean it, I really didn't, but my internal voice broke through and I just couldn't take it back. He didn't go. He did stand by me, recognising my frustration. He felt guilty.

Our split came a few weeks later. I had planned what should have been a romantic evening. I placed rose petals throughout my home. I adorned the place with candles. It was beautiful. I also prepared a lovely meal. Can I just say I am not and never have been particularly domesticated so this was a big thing for me. I opened the wine and waited for the knock at the door. It was going to be a surprise. I made a real effort but then the telephone rang and I knew it was Peter. He had been held up at work and wouldn't be able to make it down in time from Stoke where he was working. Yet another let down. I was deeply disappointed.

OK, if you date a doctor you buy into that, but this was once too often. Then again he wasn't just a hospital doctor. He was an eminent consultant. Could he not delegate? I will however be eternally grateful to him as one morning following another let down he called me. I had been feeling unwell with a raging headache. I was convinced I had something sinister wrong with me. I cried down the telephone to him. I thought I had a brain tumour. He was wonderful. He was calm. He switched from boyfriend to doctor in the blink of an eye and deduced it was unlikely to be a tumour but made me go back to be examined by my GP just in case. That kindness kept our relationship going for just that bit longer but when it finished I did feel very sad.

After Peter I dated a string of men. I had short term relationships with some wholly unsuitable people. I kept putting a plaster on the hurt in the hope it would go away. Some relationships were purely physical though a couple did have more depth, including a self-made Stockport millionaire who had a successful cosmetic company.

It's fair to add that five months after we parted Peter called me saying he had been a fool and could we start again. I should have said yes or said OK let's talk about this but instead I screamed down the telephone 'GO AWAY!' and he did. To this day I regret that. In my defence I was in a truly troubled place in my life at that time. I would love to tell you that I never made that mistake again but I did, and then deeply regretted it.

For many years my life was my work. I was a youth and community worker for Bury working in a variety of establishments with those aged from five to infinity. My strength was initiating and promoting new groups, which included a successful reminiscence group that had a fabulous collection of war time stories to recount as well as a youth drama group. I had a full programme of work there and loved it but now I needed more. I had qualified as a youth worker at Bury and was now being offered the opportunity to undertake specialist work with the Alternative Provision Project, or the APP as it was known. It was a group for those excluded from mainstream school. Some were school phobic, some had committed serious misdemeanours and some were pre-sixteen mums. Often I worked with those who had been abused or been in abusive situations, which was surreal for me but it also gave me the edge and a real empathy. I truly, truly 'felt' for them.

My manager Chris was skilled at working with young people who others gave up on. It was as though she had this special link with them. They appeared to understand each other immediately as though there was some sort of telepathic link. I admired her. In turn she valued my skills and the ability I had to explore their particular situations leading to possible solutions. I was sworn at many times but when a breakthrough came, no matter how small, the sense of satisfaction was immense.

During my time there I began attending Manchester University on a part-time basis to improve my youth work qualification. Little did I know that three months after completing my two-year course I would be an Arts Project Officer for Salford City Council and would completely leave my old world behind. On August 10th 1997 I began my new job for Salford City Council. I was stepping into a whole new world with new colleagues to become acquainted with, including Angela, my co-worker. Despite my title – arts project officer – I wore many hats. I was a counsellor, 'a sister', an advocate, a tea maker, a carer and champion of individuals and causes. It was a full-on role. I could have easily worked sixty hours a week and sometimes did.

Salford is a wonderful city whose people are the salt of the earth. There are many genuine people trying to make a living. It's not leafy like some of our South Manchester counterparts and many of the young people I worked with came from complex personal situations. The Phoenix Theatre in Pendleton was home to the Young Women's Drama Group, created to act as a vehicle to voice and explore the issues facing those aged twelve years and upwards. The work was cathartic and challenging in equal measures. Their pinnacle moment came as they rehearsed a devised piece entitled 'Girl on Girl' led by renowned theatre director Sue Reddish. She was a bright, vibrant and gifted worker and the girls loved her and her style of teaching.

'Girl on Girl' was based on an article in the Guardian newspaper at the time reporting on the increase in girl gangs. Through discussion the girls pinpointed the issues they wanted to address. They were rape, theft, family breakdowns and abuse. A few eyebrows were raised by senior management but we knew it would be done with sensitivity.

Our central character had been abused by her uncle, sending her off the rails. No one found that out until the end, when her actions made sense. The lead was only fourteen years of age. It was tough, there were tantrums. I lost count of the times girls threatened to quit during the process. Sue was fair but firm and she produced the goods. Twelve weeks later 'Girl on Girl' premiered at the Phoenix.

There wasn't a dry eye in the house. The girls performed for three nights to a packed audience. It was immensely emotional to watch. Lisa portrayed the victim of abuse with conviction and believability. It was difficult not to feel for her character, despite her horrid actions. My daughter Gemma had invited her form teacher to the opening night. He was unable to speak at the end, consumed by emotion. The actors were euphoric. Their sense of achievement had gone off the scale. They just wanted to do it again and again and again. It would have made a superb touring play for schools educating, informing and evoking strong discussion.

Present in the foyer after a performance were related organisations including Child Line NW. Lisa came to me afterwards and told me she had been approached by a young woman not many years older than herself who expressed her thanks for her portrayal of the character. She had been a victim too. The play touched so many people in different ways. How wonderful. The next two nights went equally well and the project was deemed a success, despite the initial reservations.

The Phoenix Theatre was once the famous home to the Salford Players and the acting greats Sir Ben Kingsley, Albert Finney and Robert Powell. I was in awe of a handwritten note from Albert Finney I read whilst in the lighting box. The theatre though great lacked adequate security, particularly when it came to external lighting which was usually vandalised as quickly as it was fixed. Whilst it was a superb community resource it was also a money pit. It would have been easy to feel frightened or uneasy and on at least two occasions I had good reason to feel that way. One evening some of the younger children were performing on stage. The auditorium was full of proud parents, siblings and friends. I was at the back of the auditorium when I heard banging coming from the fire exit next to the stage. Sometimes you would hear a single bang as high spirited kids ran past. This was different. It started as a short, intermittent knock. Some of the performers were a little distracted but carried on regardless.

I then overhead a couple of the parents voicing their disapproval. One dad suggested to a couple of others that he would go outside and sort it. I knew this could end badly so I quickly went into the foyer where my line manager was chatting to a guest. I walked across to Bill, our caretaker, who was behind the bar and told him I was going outside. My manager saw me leave the building. I fully expected him to follow. As I walked around the building I saw three young men around the fire exit banging on the door laughing. I turned around. I was on my own. Instinctively I just walked over to them.

If they were going to hurt me there would be no back up. As I approached I tried not to look frightened. Slowly they began to close in on me. My thoughts now turned to my children, Gemma then aged nine and Josh just four. I now realised how idiotic my decision to come outside had been. I tried to make light of the situation and retain an upbeat manner rather than yelling the odds, which would have been foolish. Incredibly, they were quite receptive. It turned out they were bored. One even said sorry. Unemployment in the area was rife. Kicks, no matter how small, gave them a buzz. This had been one of those moments. As they disbursed and I sighed I realised I had not been on my own. Bill had been present at a reasonable distance behind me. He asked me if I was all right. I smiled and nodded. Back in the foyer my manager gave me a proverbial pat on the back. Pity he didn't feel able to join us outside. Ironically the person who offered back up earned the least of all of us and was the father of four young children himself.

The next time I faced danger was during the day. The theatre had a bunch of keys that would have put Alcatraz to shame. The final key released the heavy black shutters completing the closing process. The department had a strict policy stating that when only one member of staff was present at the theatre no members of the public could be admitted.

One Thursday afternoon I was sat at a table in the theatre foyer facing the front entrance. It was my opportunity to catch up on some much needed paperwork. Thirty minutes before I was due to leave three young men in their late teens appeared at the door. They may well have been the same three from the fire door incident but I couldn't swear to it. Wearing dark clothing one beckoned me to the front door. I hesitated for a moment. I stood up and walked over to them. A through-the-glass conversation took place. The lad in the centre wanted to know if there was a toilet he could use. He was polite and quite possibly genuine in his request. I politely explained there was but that I was unable to let them in due to company policy.

"Come on. I only want to use the toilet." Once again I repeated the rule. There was a thud on the glass. A little group chatter then the lads dispersed. I decided it was wise to wait a while longer before beginning to close up, to allow them time to leave. I left it fifteen minutes then peered through the large glass frontage. There was no one about. I started to lock the internal doors which took seven or eight minutes. I then put on my jacket, picked up my paperwork and opened the front door. The coast was clear. I confidently stepped outside turning my back to lock the door before activating the shutter. The process took no more than a couple of minutes and as the shutter reached the floor I crouched down to check it had locked in place. As I stood up and turned around those three young men were face to face with me. Well they would have been had we been the same height. Here we go again, I thought. I was holding my breath waiting for at best a torrent of abuse and at worse, well that didn't bear thinking about.

"I really did only want to use the toilet. You could have let us in."

"I know but I could have lost my job if I had. I am sorry," I replied, wondering if they would let me off with my pathetic-sounding excuse. Once again, I got my reprieve. They left and I hurried to my car.

Working with the Salford community gave me some special moments. The young women's group made me burst with pride. My other success was a consumer rights group – women using drama to gain confidence. I was also running a school outreach programme fleshing out a peer mentor programme for those working with individuals who had been bullied, which proved so successful that the Principal of Salford College asked if I would run an anti-bullying programme with his college tutors alongside weekly work within the PSE programmes.

My work was burgeoning but so was my depression, a condition I had fought relentlessly for a number of years. Attitudes to depression are different now. It's a condition that's talked about. In the late nineties it was still a taboo subject with a stigma to match. Back at the office I shared with my co-worker Angela our relationship was becoming increasingly strained. I found it ironic I was co-ordinating a successful anti-bullying programme outside of the office but could not deal with the worker who had bullied me since day one of my job there. My line manager appeared to do very little to deal with the situation. I would often find a moment and a space and literally break down, then compose myself for my next appointment. Soon I began blocking my working world out. I wasn't listening to the people I worked with or my colleagues. Once again, I was on the outside looking in.

My world was very blurry. I knew I could no longer carry on like this. It was tough because I really cared about the community I worked with and my projects. There was just so much work for me to do. Senior management were concerned and in time I was referred to the company doctor. I tried to put on a brave face with him. I played down the problem. It was as though the more serious the situation was the more I made light of it. He saw through this and after a subsequent consultation at the age of thirty-five I was retired on health grounds. My GP was fantastic and very supportive. Without his support I fear I would have gone under. My glittering career was now well and truly over. What on earth was I going to do next?

CHAPTER EIGHT

SECOND CHANCES

I needed a fresh start. I took time out in an attempt to recover, repair and reframe. A whole new world beckoned. I had been considering career options for some time. Perhaps I could retrain? Initially I chose a part-time law degree at Manchester University. I had aspirations to be a barrister. They were actors after all, convincing their audience or in this case the jury. A few months in however I realised just how boring those early years of study would be. Clearly I must have had a low boredom threshold. I decided I didn't have enough of a desire to apply myself to study for an extended period of time and made the decision to leave. I never regretted it.

I had time with the children. That was a novelty. I had returned to work when Gemma was three months old and similarly with Josh. Gemma was nine now. She was doing well at school. She too had a desire to follow a career path within the arts. A sensible girl who was forthright and bossy at times. I knew she could fight her corner intelligently if a situation warranted it. We were more alike than I cared to admit. We were very close at that time. The strong mother/daughter bond appeared impenetrable. I knew that in the event something happened to me she could forge a path for herself, do well and be there for her brother as well.

One evening I came close to her finding that out when an accident occurred on the busy M60 motorway. A strange series of events occurred in the lead up to the accident, which began at a car dealership a few days before. I went to test drive a BMW with a friend. It was a three series in Techno Violet and I loved it, to the pleasure of the salesman. When we got back to the dealership I was itching to sign the paperwork for my dream car. My friend however suggested I walk away. Walk away? But I wanted it. "Go away and call him tomorrow if you like, but just take some time to think it through." Reluctantly I did just that, muttering under my breath as I did.

I was going to visit a friend that evening in Prestbury, which is an affluent area of Cheshire with more millionaires per square foot than anywhere else. I didn't drink and drive. In fact I had drunk nothing more than sparkling water all evening – thankfully. Driving back on the M60 heading for the Worsley turn off in my trusted Fiat Punto I suddenly felt sleepy. It was as though someone had drugged me. The sensation lasted for seconds. I shook my head and carried on driving. I was so close to my exit. It was a Sunday evening, almost eleven pm. The roads were a little wet. The motorway was full. I remember the supermarket artic taking its load alongside those I suspected were returning home like me. I switched the radio on and opened the window a little. It happened again. In fact it happened three times, only it wasn't third time lucky for me. I had swerved across three lanes and was careering into the central reservation barrier. Whilst I do not advocate this as I way of waking yourself up it most certainly did. This was the one and only time where I wasn't on the outside looking in. As the car was crashing out of control I said goodbye in my head to my children and anyone close to me at that time. Fortunately the children were with Barbara, the child minder. I desperately tried to swerve the car away from the barrier thinking I would probably be hit at any second. As I concentrated on gripping the steering wheel, trying desperately to regain control of the vehicle, I was immediately drawn to the front passenger seat. 'Someone' or 'something' had appeared in the car mid-accident. They were most evidently there and clearly not from the physical realm. Up until that point I had been panicking, waiting for my final moment. As the car began spinning back to the other side of the carriageway I felt an immense calm. It was like a massive worry being washed away, like a wave of morphine. I guessed my passenger was with me to either save me or accompany me to the next life. Either way I was no longer frightened. After what felt like hours but was clearly only seconds my car slammed into the near-side barrier, bringing it to a dramatic halt. At that point I was most definitely on my own. Whoever or whatever had appeared in the car had only been brought in for the final part of the accident. It was dark and very quiet. Was I dead or had I been spared?

A few moments later a softly spoken female voice called out "Are you OK?" I honestly believed it was an angel. In reality a couple had pulled up behind me, having seen what had happened. I was indeed ALIVE. How could I have survived on such a busy stretch of carriageway? As the police vehicle arrived I turned to look at the motorway. I vividly remember seeing three full lanes of traffic yet during my accident crossing three lanes and back again not one single, solitary vehicle was on there. It didn't make sense.

I firmly believe my guardian angel had been brought in to stop the traffic at the point of most danger. My car was a write off yet I walked away without a scratch. Do I believe in divine intervention? You bet I do. As I sat in the police vehicle sipping coffee awaiting the recovery truck I realised just how lucky I had been. It could so easily have gone the other way. I was badly shaken but I was most definitely alive.

I've tried many times over the years to make sense of that night but my conclusion is always the same. It just wasn't my time. I firmly believe our life book has a designated number of pages. When you get to the last page that's it. You can't magic up any more no matter how much you would like to. On a visit to the locum GP at my surgery next day he was amazed I had sustained nothing more than muscle stiffness and mild whiplash. I'm not sure he believed I had been in a motorway smash, but my now defunct car was living proof of the traumatic events of the previous evening.

Having always considered myself to have a psychic awareness and experienced phenomena I considered this to be a message to open my door to the psychic world rather than ignoring it, which I duly did and still do to this day. Had I not been in my tank of a Punto I could have been in the BMW I was going to buy and perhaps not been so lucky. The police officer said: "That car saved your life. It took the brunt of what should have happened to you." How lucky had I been?

Not long after the accident a new GP came to my practice, Dr Kyaw, who to this day has steered me through some very bad times and helped to rationalise my thoughts. He is without a doubt the best doctor I have ever had.

In the year 2000 I retrained in holistic therapies. I devoted myself wholeheartedly to study and practical application. I loved it and I excelled at it too, being the first student in my year to be allowed to work on living, breathing clients. Holistic therapy for all its techniques and associated products has a real, whole, centred and spiritual approach to it which acted as a calming influence on me at a time when I really needed it.

Not wanting to lose my arts roots and in complete contradiction to my therapies I decided to set up Bright Sparks – a TV casting agency which primarily put children forward for work. If anything life became more not less stressful. No sooner had we taken our first steps than we were approached by a French TV director asking us for children and adults to take part in a TV commercial for Umbro France. This was to be our baptism of fire. Could I deliver? I would give it a damn good try. I found forty children and adults to attend a casting at a Manchester hotel. There were people kicking footballs everywhere. It was a success. We did it. We had just the right mix of adults and children to satisfy the company. We secured the contract. I had secured the contract.

A year later the success continued when we supplied the lead actors for a feature film shot in Manchester who appeared alongside well-known actors. More success came as a number of kids were cast in popular television shows across the networks, leading to the creation of a theatre school in Eccles. As the first school opened and we held an Open Evening prospective pupils and their parents continually streamed through the doors. It was unbelievable but I believe there was a real need at that time for quality training provided by my competent team. I discovered a terrier-like instinct. I held on doggedly to concepts and ideas that others doubted would work, including teaching staff some of whom I clashed with and then subsequently parted company with. If I believed in something I went for it whether that be a person, a concept or a project. Nothing worse than thinking 'what if?', rather do it and fail than never do it at all.

Eccles Masonic Hall hosted us for five years before we secured a unit at Bridgewater Mill. Bright Sparks became an extended family to me, perhaps the family I wished I'd had. It was difficult not to feel pride. Frustration usually came via the parents who wanted their children to secure auditions or get the lead parts in productions. I realised being honest wasn't always what they wanted to hear but I carried on regardless, clashing with a number of parents along the way. As the song goes '*I did it my way*'. This is a precarious industry with absolutely no guarantees. I always believed the best parents are those who support from the sidelines offering lots of encouragement along the way.

I always remember an exceedingly pushy parent who pushed her daughter and me endlessly. In the early days of the agency I spent almost forty minutes four times a week on the telephone to her. I tried to be polite but it was difficult and I was naive. Mum alienated directors with her over-the-top manner. If the truth be known she lost her daughter some chances because of it. One day a producer from Monkey Television asked if I had any pushy parents. Only one came to mind. When I mentioned the mother's name I was told her name had been given by FOUR other agencies! I rest my case.

Bright Sparks made me very proud. There were some exceptional actors and staff. Lea, my vocal coach and one half of the duo '*Sweet Female Attitude*', was my most loyal and most talented. When Bright Sparks Academy came to an end in 2008 I was left with many happy memories. I wept as I carefully peeled the photographic images of our time together from the walls. This was now the time to re-evaluate my life path. Little did I know where it would lead.

A parent once commented in a less-than-tactful manner that

I may have forgotten what it was like to attend an audition. She was possibly right in her observation. If ever there was a time to start attending them then it was now. Cue auditions. At first I applied for auditions like everyone else. The successful ones included: ITV *Golden Balls*, BBC *Weakest Link* and Channel 4 *Quiz Trippers*. I got through the early rounds of *Big Brother* but failed at *Who Wants to be a Millionaire?* I was at least getting asked to attend. I then secured an agent who sent me to auditions as and when required. Was this the new beginning I wanted and needed or might other elements interfere?

CHAPTER NINE

LOVE AND HATE

The year 2008 was a landmark for me for both good and bad reasons, though more bad than good if I'm honest. One afternoon I caught a TV interview with an actor I had never really noticed before. Then, suddenly I did, if you know what I mean. I watched his interview with interest. He had really captured my eye. For legal reasons I cannot reveal his true identity but for the purpose of this book I will refer to him as 'James'.

As a TV agent there were some perks. One was that my role as a TV casting agent gave me some gravitas when approaching fellow artistes with work enquiries. They usually at least read correspondence or their agent passed it onto them for their consideration. It didn't however guarantee a reply and this was not a business introduction after all. It was a tricky communication but I knew I just had to take that chance if I was to make contact with him.

James had a successful career on both sides of the Atlantic. He had just left a popular TV show and was now on tour with a play. Better still the tour would be coming to a theatre near me so I penned a friendly introduction informing him I was planning on seeing the play and would he like to meet up afterwards. Posting that letter was to be a truly fateful moment. It was a moment that would change my life forever. My mouth was dry. My heart was racing. What had I just done? I didn't know this man. I had never taken any interest in him or his career previously so why now? Was this a psychic intervention moment? Was I meant to send this letter?

A couple of days passed by which point other things were pre-occupying my thoughts, namely work. I had bought the tickets to see the play in a week's time and would go whether I received a response or not. I had invited a teenage actor to accompany me. She was achieving success herself in a long-running show. A play should be shared and she deserved the treat. A week passed by. It was the day of the play. Having received no reply I resigned myself to not meeting him. Oh well, it wasn't meant to be, I thought. As I scurried around attending to my 'to do' list I heard the message tone bleep on my mobile. I reached for it and clicked the message icon. It was from an unfamiliar number. As I opened the message I realised it was from him. It was from 'James'. He had read my letter and seen my photograph of which I had joked about not having two heads. His text read: "It would be a delight to meet you and even if you do have two heads one at least is beautiful. James."

I was euphoric. I felt like I had won the lottery. This was ludicrous. I was about to meet an actor many women would have given their right arm to meet. I felt like a lovesick teenager. I managed to compose myself – just. Seeing his name at the bottom of the text made it very real. He suggested we meet in the theatre bar after the performance. I replied almost immediately agreeing to his offer.

As I collected Izzy, my companion for the evening, the weather was taking a turn for the worse. High winds were building. Going to the coast would be fun then. News reports advised against visiting coastal areas and here we were heading straight for the eye of the storm.

As we arrived we battled against the winds to keep upright. Within a few minutes we both looked completely dishevelled. As we had time to spare I took Izzy to KFC for a bite to eat. She wolfed down her chicken and chips and guzzled happily on her coca cola. I on the other hand couldn't face any of mine and I shoved my food towards Izzy who happily ate it. My stomach was fighting with itself and didn't appear to be winning either. I looked at the time. We needed to be heading for the theatre. I went to the bathroom to make myself a little more presentable, which was to be a complete waste of time as within minutes of leaving I looked totally unkempt again.

We arrived at the theatre and took to our seats. As the safety curtain rose I saw James scan the audience using only his eyes in an attempt, I assume, to look out for me. It is a consummate professional who can do that. Perhaps he thought I wouldn't turn up. Maybe he was just as excited about meeting me as I was at meeting him. I can honestly say I never digested any of the play. I was for some reason preoccupied!

As the final bow was taken and the safety curtain fell Izzy and I headed to the theatre bar. A gust of wind hit us as we walked the hundred yards or so to the bar. I quickly tried to straighten myself up. I took a deep breath as we opened the door to the bar. I peered around. I was thankful it was quiet in there but I knew that would change as everyone headed there after the performance.

As the weather was stormy the bar remained quiet. James's co-star arrived first and headed over to the bar with a friend. He passed me a cursory glance. Perhaps James had asked him to check me out and text him if he was at all concerned. I needn't have worried. The bar door opened and James arrived clutching a red gift bag which he left near the door. I assumed it was a gift from a fan. He looked a little hot and a bit dishevelled if I'm honest but it was a thrill none the less. It wasn't too difficult to spot us in the empty bar. He quickly spotted me and smiled. My heart melted. He had the most amazing blue eyes. He gave me a peck on both cheeks before asking us what we wanted to drink.

I had chosen our seating carefully. I opted for a corner table with an 'L'-shaped bench seat. James came over with the drinks and sat next to me. In fact he sat so close his leg was almost glued to mine. He totally did it for me. Within minutes

I was at ease in his company but chose my words carefully none the less. Be cool I told myself. Easier said than done I thought. We chatted about our work, the play and Izzy's role in her TV series. A long time actor friend of his was in the show so they found plenty to talk about. She asked him if he found it difficult to cry as an actor. He said men often did find it more difficult so he would use a tear stick. The night wore on. Before long it was time to go. As Izzy went to the toilet it was my chance to say 'thank you' privately. I had quickly left my casting agent hat by the wayside. As we kissed each other on the cheek I assumed there would be no further contact. I made the decision not to contact him unless he contacted me. It had been a wonderful evening.

The following afternoon I received a text from him expressing his thanks for meeting him. It was an unexpected but welcome surprise none the less. The text opened the door to a dialogue. James would take me to every emotion over the course of the next few months. I would love and hate him simultaneously at times. Not only was he a temperamental man he was also a married one. I surmised it wasn't a happy marriage or that it was perhaps a marriage in name only.

Over time James took me to the height of ecstasy then plummeting right back down to the depths of despair. We argued more than we laughed. At times we were as close as we were distant. He could be overbearing but he could be immensely caring too. I knew as his tour neared its end meeting up as we had been doing would be difficult. We lived in different parts of the country. I made the mistake women make up and down the country. I put a man on a pedestal. He meant the world to me. If he snapped his fingers I would jump. I always seemed to put myself out far more than him. I was losing control again.

I will be honest. I don't make a good 'other woman'. I'm too selfish for that. I didn't want to share him for a start but I had slipped into the role without realising it. I told myself I was in control but I wasn't. His moods were mega difficult. When it was good it was great. When it was bad it was very bad. It was as though he had two buttons for me. One was like a huge magic plaster that soothed and restored me whilst the other took me to the darkest of places and he held the remote.

He had a punishing work schedule. I commented very early on that he should ease back a little, which is never a popular comment to make to a working actor. The remark struck a chord with him. He replied that he might soon have to. I didn't take too much notice of the comment though perhaps I should have done. I was so pleased to spend time in his company but he was so often pre-occupied when with me. My friend Lynn thought I was an idiot. She interfered too much sometimes. My daughter deeply disapproved of him. She overheard me arguing with him and saw how upset I was. We fell out a lot. I was viewing him through rose-tinted glasses I know that. Those closest to me could see that too. I know they didn't want me to get hurt but I was in this for the long term. Maybe I could give him a child. Wouldn't that be the ultimate gift a woman could give a man?

One night we had arranged to meet after his play. It had been a difficult day. It wasn't destined to improve either. I turned up to meet him at the wrong place, which was an hour and a half away. The hotel chain we had arranged to meet at was also local to me. As I pulled up in the car park and sent him a text to say I had arrived it dawned on me I was not where I was supposed to be. He called. He was angry. He had rushed from the theatre to meet me. I was weepy. I always played second fiddle to his tune. These were merely snatched moments with a married man. Then add the celebrity tag to the mix and it becomes impossible.

We ended up having a row over the telephone. We were both very emotional. Crossed words were exchanged but nothing would prepare me for what came next. The man I had come to care about so very much was dying. He had terminal cancer. He blurted it out in temper. "I'm fucking dying," he yelled. "What?" I could instantly feel the blood draining from me. Did he just say what I think he said? It's not often I am lost for words but I was now. Did he know all of this when he met me? Why did he become close to me? Was I to be his distraction? Sometimes there are no words. Well, none that will make a difference. From that moment on he did everything he could to push me away. He yelled. He shouted. He was downright unpleasant. I was in utter turmoil. For the first time in my life I had met a man I truly loved. I had met my soul mate.

Instead of pushing me away his news drew me closer. His drawbridge was closing whilst I was desperately trying to slide back under before it shut forever. He must have been so scared. Here was a strong, strapping man. He didn't look ill. He could walk faster down a high street than me. Perhaps he was lying. Maybe he wasn't ill after all. If I was a play toy then he was bored with me. So many things were running through my head and not all of them were nice. My whole world had come crashing down around me.

At that point my relationship with Gemma started to suffer too. I was blaming anyone who disapproved of us. Well, it started with her but ultimately I blamed James. Why had he let me get close to him when he knew how ill he was? That was selfish. Then to push me away once he had told me was the ultimate insult. I was angry. I wanted to love James but I hated him too.

During his last week on tour we met for lunch in a very dark pub/tavern which would not have been out of place in *Les Miserables*. He was totally horrible to me. He was bullying me in an attempt to find out why I was being so horrible to him. He was like a man on a mission. He just wouldn't give up. I was being interrogated. The tears flowed like never before. I kept looking at the carpet. I couldn't look at him. My emotions were very raw yet he continued to pound me with the same line of questioning. So I answered him. "I'm hitting you with words because you're dying and you are too young to die." There. I'd said it. As I looked up at his face his eyes were brimming with tears. He was clearly choked up. He couldn't speak. Clearly, if nothing else he now knew how much I cared and how concerned I was. I hoped we would reach out to each other. I wanted to but he didn't or couldn't.

That was the toughest day. I felt like the lowest of the low. Where was my compassion? Why could I not be more understanding? It was because I couldn't deal with the enormity of the situation. As we parted company that day I fully intended to break away, for my sanity as much as for his. That's what he wanted after all but three weeks later I was in contact again. As I sent him a text I discovered he was in the car with his wife. She had picked up his mobile phone and realised this text wasn't from a business associate. From that moment on it became nothing short of horrific. I was hopelessly in love with a dying man who was married who was desperately pushing me away. I wanted to die.

A couple of weeks later my friend Lynn called me. Had I seen the double page spread of him with his wife? Clearly, they had made up or were perhaps giving the impression to the world they had. I was livid. I called him. I was hurting. He told me she had in fact kicked him out of the house. Now he would never forgive me. I had lost the love of my life.

CHAPTER TEN

BLACK CLOUD

At 7.00pm on a Sunday evening in late October 2008 I sat in my office at home at the computer. I wrote 'I am sorry. Please forgive me. I love you both. Mum xx' I left the page open on the screen. It was my goodbye to my two lovely children.

I had been in a state for the previous few hours. I was in turmoil and deeply depressed. Gemma was desperately worried and angry with me too in the way you are when someone you love is out of reach. We had rowed. The atmosphere was strained. Gemma was upstairs with her boyfriend Sam. They were both home from university for the holidays. Josh was in his room on the Play Station. I could slip away quietly, unnoticed. I found it difficult to hold back the tears. As I turned off the light in the office the computer monitor glowed with my message only a click away. I turned for a moment to look to the top of the landing where my children were. They were no doubt pre-occupied with their own activities. I could now slip away almost unnoticed.

It's important to make sure your make up is right. I took extra care touching it up. I powdered my nose, cheeks and forehead a little before applying, blotting and reapplying my lipstick. I was wearing a red zip-up top which was complimented by a vibrant red lipstick. I took great care of my appearance. I always have done. I overcompensate for my insecurities by looking as good as I possibly can.

Driving to Salford Quays my mind was in a blur. It was like driving with a knitted fog blanket in front of me but unlike a demister I could not wipe it away. It just sat there shrouding me. I took a number of deep breaths on that journey. I battled with the tears. My life was flashing by in front of me. I smiled a little as I recalled the fun times with the children. There was the trip to Disney World with what appeared to be a hearing-impaired rabbit from *Alice in Wonderland!* Then I remembered the whistle-stop trip we made to a European Christmas market and the deep fried cauliflower delicacy I just couldn't quite stomach. There were so many happy memories, but at that moment I struggled to hold onto them long enough to change my mind set and turn the car around.

As I arrived at the Quays I had a decision to make. Where would be the best place to park. Should I stay near the entrance with lots of passing traffic or do I head to the far end of the Quays and a more discreet spot? It was relatively congested that evening so I ended up at the quieter end by default. A lot of the area was pedestrianised so available parking was limited. Eventually I chose a spot at the rear of an estate agent which had just three parking spaces. I felt snug and safe there. I was cold. It was a chilly night. I blasted on the heaters in the four-by-four and left the engine running. I took a sip of water before checking my lipstick again. I then ran a brush through my blonde hair. In my handbag were letters I had written, including one for my children just in case they didn't see the computer message. There was also one for James and one for a reporter friend of mine. It's important to leave answers to some of those questions that may be asked afterwards. I tried my best to do that in the letters I had written. I then placed them neatly on the dashboard. I then sent James a text knowing he would be on stage when it was received.

I carried a large handbag which was always full of everything and nothing. There were lipsticks, foundation, tissues, hairbrush, endless receipts, odd sweets, bottled water and the three packets of aspirin I had bought at the garage near my home. At that point in my life I believed that I was nothing more than a liability to those I loved. I was experiencing a whirlwind of conflicting emotions. I had got used to bottling everything up. It was easier than alarming people. I was frightened to go and see my GP in case he thought I was mad or something. I had visions of him arranging for me to be sectioned.

I stared at the packets of aspirin. My plan was to take them packet by packet, knowing that as I slipped out of consciousness someone would eventually find me and alert my family. I toyed with the packet a couple of times. I picked them up once or twice before promptly putting them back in my bag. I just needed a moment to think. Finding clarity was difficult. I did try to consider the feelings of the people who would be left behind and their lasting memory of me. Would they hate me? They would certainly be hurt by my actions and angry with me. Perhaps one day they might understand. Had the shoe been on the other foot I would not understand. You see it's not about the person that goes it's about those left behind who are hurt, confused and bewildered by their loved one's actions. I sat for a few moments and thought about that before reaching into my bag once again, taking out the water and a packet of tablets. As I popped out the first tablet from the foil packet and swallowed it I knew the process had begun. Do you leave the tablets to settle in your stomach or do you just constantly pop them in one after the other? It's not the sort of question you ask, is it? I then took a couple more. As I reached for my next I heard a voice in my head telling me to call for help. It came from nowhere. It was a loud, definite command. It was a man's voice. Was this some sort of telepathic message from James?

I then remember dialling the number for Greater Manchester Police and not the 999 number. I didn't feel like I was a priority. I felt more like an encumbrance. A male police officer answered.

"Hello, Greater Manchester Police. Can I help you?"

I hesitated. What the hell do you say? I stuttered a little then apologised.

"That's OK. Take your time. What's your name?"

"Audrey."

"Audrey. OK, how can I help you?"

What followed was incoherent garbage. I was emotional. I felt the need to rush. I felt like I was wasting this man's time. There was probably somebody out there who really needed their help. I swear he sensed how I was feeling and said quite calmly,

"Take your time."

He then went on to ask if he could send an officer to my home to speak to me. I told him I wasn't at home. I was at Salford Quays. He was very calm but I could hear him typing very fast in the background.

I told him that James had cancer and that I couldn't cope with knowing that. He asked if I had cancer. No, it was James who had it. He kept me talking for a few minutes. I can't tell you what he said at that point but it was clearly conversation that required a response and therefore kept me on the telephone just that bit longer. He was really skilled at that. It was that wonderful officer and him alone who prevented me from taking more tablets. It's easier to talk to a stranger, especially when they are trained to listen and respond accordingly. The next thing I knew I had cut him off. I panicked. I had a plan but I had been side-tracked. I needed a moment to think the situation through. I had off loaded a lot to that officer. My mouth was dry. My heart was racing. I took a sip of water. I then saw a lone police officer fastening up his jacket. It was very chilly out there. He was walking in my direction. We glanced at each other but he walked past. Clearly applying my make up properly had the desired effect. I did not raise any suspicions and he carried on walking to the end of the Quays. I just knew it was me he was looking for.

Sometimes you are granted a moment of clarity where you realise the enormity of your actions. Did I really want to die or did I want someone to listen and not judge? I surmised that if I did want to die I wasn't brave enough to carry it through. I was so cold. I shivered as I turned the key in the ignition and set off away from the Quays. As I drove home I figured I could if it came to it take my tablets when I went to bed and then I would die the coward's way – in my sleep.

I pulled onto the drive. I slipped in quietly and headed straight for bed. I felt drained both emotionally and physically. It was like the stuffing had been knocked out of me. I undressed and climbed into my nice warm bed. I pulled the duvet right up to my chin. I wanted to cocoon myself. I was sleepy, very sleepy. Perhaps I wouldn't wake up. If I had wanted to consume more tablets at that point I did not have the energy to administer them. Had I taken more tablets than I thought? I quickly fell asleep. When I awoke next morning the cloud of depression that hung over me for so long was heavy and ominous. I felt awful but I was alive.

When I came downstairs the look on Josh's face said it all. He had seen the message I had left on the computer screen the night before. Gemma was angry with me. She didn't understand and I could not explain. They knew nothing of the events of the previous evening and to this day I have never told them. Why upset them any further? I knew the writing was on the wall in terms of my relationship with Gemma, which was already at breaking point. She was rightly exasperated with me. She must have felt so helpless. I needed her to understand the torturous effect James and his illness was having on me but at that time she didn't. She couldn't. Thank God she had Sam for support.

A short time later she went back to University with Sam. It was a strained goodbye. It would be Christmas before I saw her again, which was to prove to be a catalyst for our ever-growing rift.

The weeks went by and I limped along. It was now nearly Christmas. I was feeling very down. Gemma arrived home alone for the holidays. Sam would follow on a couple of days later. I was pleased to see her. I was very proud of her. But before long our catch-up conversation brought us around to the thorny subject of James. I needed to make her understand. I wanted her to appreciate the emotional agony I was enduring. I tried to talk about him but it was like showing a red rag to a bull every time I mentioned his name. Eventually my frustration got the better of me and an argument ensued. I blurted out that I had tried to take my own life and apparently implied it was her fault for not being more supportive and understanding. I yelled at her. "If you can't offer me that support then get out."

As I left her in her bedroom I expected the dust to settle between us then the odd word would be uttered before we started to talk again. It was Boxing Day. I was her Mum.

An hour or so later she came down the stairs carrying her bags. She had tears streaming down her face. She was leaving. I was angry that she didn't understand. She wasn't a baby. She was a grown woman. At that point I should have apologised profusely to her but I couldn't. Her father pulled up in his car and she left. I did call her. She told me I blamed her for wanting to take my own life. She wanted an apology, but like her I am stubborn. I couldn't give her the apology she wanted. As the days turned into weeks I tried to make contact with her again, giving obscure reasons for contact. This was my way of holding out the olive branch. I knew she was waiting for me to say 'sorry' and I was in my own way. I just couldn't give her the words she wanted and needed.

The weeks became months and soon it was the following Christmas and twelve months had passed. Mother's Day came and went without a call, a text or a card. That hurt. As the months passed I resigned myself to the fact that I had lost my daughter. As I write this we are still not in contact, four years later.

In a funny sort of way it's as though things are back to normal without being normal, if that makes sense. We were so close once. Nothing would have parted us, but James did. I resented him for his illness but also for the parting with my beloved daughter. My life was a mess, I was a mess. Once again I had destroyed a valued relationship, underpinning the realisation that I experience a relief when a relationship finishes and I no longer face the pressure of keeping people happy. It's a coping mechanism. Why then could I not break that link with James and experience that same relief? That might just have saved my relationship with my daughter. I was trapped like a frightened rabbit with nowhere to run and no one to turn to. Had I have known the sequence of events that would occur as a result of posting that letter I would never have sent it. So, be careful what or who you wish for as you might just get it.

CHAPTER ELEVEN

STILL FIGHTING

By now you may well have made your mind up about me. You may have decided that I am damaged and you would be right. You may think it silly to hold out for love no matter what the cost and the cost here has been huge. You may even have your own opinions about my involvement with a married man. Perhaps you are reading this and have been in a similar situation yourself. Maybe you are a silent survivor. Whatever your opinion of me I have always tried to see the best in other people. My expectations are high and I do expect a lot from others, perhaps too much at times. When someone lets me down I do tend to take it personally.

Someone out there should create a list of formula to be applied to the various area of one's life, a list where you can find the correct formula for the perfect solution. I think that's been invented already, it's called a magic wand ....

I am conscious of coming across as the harbourer of doom and gloom. Whilst I can't change what's happened thus far it is important as the reader to know I have had a lot of fun times during my life too, though being thrown into the swimming pool as a non-swimmer at Butlins wasn't one of them!

Holidays with the children have provided me with some much cherished moments which are all the more precious now. I recall the three of us standing at Ground Zero to remember those who perished in the 9/11 disaster, a truly moving experience and only eight months after the tragedy occurred. I have marvelled at the Art Institute in Chicago, been to the very top of Sears Tower and seen John Lennon's signature in the guest book there. I have kissed most of the Disney characters at Disney World in Florida and swam with Tyler – the most delinquent dolphin at Discovery Cove. I've danced the square tango and even have some flying hours under my belt.

Whilst this might be hard to believe I am a happy, bubbly person. I am sure there are those that would whole heartedly agree with this. Acquaintances would certainly confirm this. I have a somewhat dry sense of humour and a mischievous smile typical of a child of Mercury. I leave an impression on people for the good and for the bad. On a good day I embrace life. As a person I give far, far more than I take. I feel deeply for others and often champion the underdog.

I constantly try to forget my past. I don't want to be a victim. I am a survivor like many, many others. It is so very difficult to forget the past. I thank the media for highlighting our plight and continuing to do so. Everyone remembers the high-profile allegations but please don't forget the ordinary people who have suffered. There are many of us. Just because our abuser wasn't a celebrity doesn't make it any less significant. We too have suffered for many, many years in some cases.

I thought long and hard before telling my story and relinquishing my anonymity, but in the end the decision was an easy one. I wrote '*Outside Looking In*' to inform you, the reader, and as therapy for myself. The details of some events are scant in places but perhaps that's because I would prefer to talk about my experiences in person. I want to inspire others. I want to explore coping methods and share a platform with others who have suffered.

Abusers do not have a post-it note on their forehead telling you they are abusers. Instead they mingle amongst us. They are the man or woman on the street. My father came across as a helpful, amiable character to everyone other than us. We saw through him. He even fooled his own brother. It's as though abusers may over compensate for their horrid actions by pretending to be the perfect person to the outside world.

It was tough for me in 2008/2009 but I found my spirit and my innate dislike of injustice when I tried to save our local Advertiser newspaper from closure. The Advertiser gave so much support to Bright Sparks. I poured my heart and soul into saving a lynchpin of the local Eccles community and the jobs of front counter staff. What started as one afternoon a week quickly turned into two days and then three. The reception area became the campaign office. I spoke to as many visitors as I could who came in. A petition quickly gained three thousand signatures, but in the end we just couldn't save it. I openly wept. I felt like I had let the community down and I know what it is like to be let down by someone I relied on.

My agent in the meantime was putting me forward for TV work. In 2011 I auditioned for a TV pilot 'Quiz Trippers' following a group of strangers travelling across Scotland in a camper van taking part in nightly pub quizzes. To my amazement I was selected to take part. I threw myself into the task in hand – well, for the first twenty-four hours anyway, then living with strangers in a camper van got to all of us. Friction between us was evident and the editing suite had a field day. Scotland is truly stunning. The locals were lovely towards us. The crew were supportive. The experience was like no other and it was work. James died shortly before filming started. I was grieving for him and not in the right place to take part in the project, but I'm glad I did.

My work in therapies was going well with all manner of people having treatments including I am pleased to say medical professionals. I find it funny when one of them asks me how they are shaping up. They know I can be relied upon to be honest! Psychic readings occur in cycles. Cycles imposed by me as emotionally they take a lot out of me. I get a lot of positive feedback from my readings and a high accuracy rate. If I can help others with my readings then so be it. Talking of readings, I visited my local spiritualist church for six months solidly where I offered readings in open circle sessions. This was my way of giving something back. The only problem was that my 'companions' followed me home, meaning I was unable to switch off and making my home more like a hotel. I would be working in my office when I would hear the footsteps and voices of my uninvited guests. There is one guest however who turns up periodically. I call him my psychic bodyguard. He is a heavy-set individual who appears in shadow form. He's always in a rush. He doesn't frighten me, usually appearing to cross one landing to the next in our three-storey property. I do feel protected. I do believe in guardian angels and talk to mine. I ask for their help for others as well as myself. When I hurt someone I often speak to my angel. Goodness knows I've hurt so, so many. I would like to say sorry to anyone I've behaved unreasonably towards. I particularly want to say sorry to Peter and James, dear James.

I fear that when my day comes there will be no-one by my graveside to mourn me because I have pushed them all away. That preys on my mind. Writing my account is therapy for me. Putting my thoughts on paper crystallises events. In the confusion I've found some clarity. My faults are evident. My father left a legacy in terms of anger which I inherited. I know I have a short fuse but I do try to rein it in. I labour the point in heated discussion. I don't let it drop. I do not intentionally set out to hurt anyone but I appear to end up doing just that, which I then deeply regret. That little girl remains within me needing as much understanding and love as she ever did. I feel her reach out. I see her stamp her feet and I see and feel her tears. No child should ever suffer like that. The system let us all down.

My continued wish is to be healthy, happy and at peace. I want the demon of abuse to go away and leave me forever. Abuse destroys lives. Not just for the victim but for those around them. No one should ever feel alone. If you are reading this and are a victim then find it within yourself to speak up. My father is no longer here to face up to what he did, but there are many out there whose abusers are still alive. Use all the resources available to you to get you through. Take your frustrations out through an activity you enjoy. Ask for professional help. Most of all don't bottle up your feelings. If that means venting at others then so be it. You are entitled to be selfish. If that means you spend the next few days apologising then do it. ChildLine and others like it do a wonderful job. Thank God there are people out there who will listen and believe. I want to ask readers to disclose. Don't hold on to the heavy weight of secrecy. It achieves nothing. Let's take the stigma of abuse away. Once you tell one other person the effect ever so slightly loses its grip. As adults it's so, so difficult to disclose events that make you feel ashamed, particularly if people around you, those closest, are unaware, but that's what I am doing here and if I can do it so can you.

When I started out on this journey I didn't want to just share my experience of abuse and its effects, but the reality is it has overshadowed my life and shaped the way I think and feel and interact with others. I cannot hold down a relationship which frustrates me. I am essentially now a loner. Next time someone yells at you or appears to behave unreasonably take a moment to ask yourself why. Are they just having a bad day or is there a more serious underlying reason?

I am using my final chapter to tell you about a campaign I have initiated entitled 'IT'S OK'. It represents the many silent survivors who for whatever reason feel unable to speak up. It has a simple message 'Tell one other person and lighten your load'. IT'S OK to speak up. I appeal to anyone who has suffered abuse to step forward, whether you be the girl next door or a more high-profile figure yourself. By telling one other person you begin the fight-back process and abuse loosens its grip on you. Try it. It's a liberating process.

My final words are those of thanks and by way of an apology to my children and to the professionals who have helped me over the years, with special thanks to my GP Dr Kyaw, who over the years has helped me more than he knows. Thank you. All of you.